Vanishing

ALSO BY CANDIDA LAWRENCE

Fear Itself

Change of Circumstance

Reeling & Writhing

CANDIDA LAWRENCE   *Vanishing*

UNBRIDLED
BOOKS

Unbridled Books

Copyright 2009 by Candida Lawrence
Some pieces in this volume were originally published, as follows:
"The Day I Saw My Parents Naked" (the first section of "We're All in This Together), *Cache Review*, 1984
"Based on Experience," *Berkeley Poets Cooperative*, 1985
"What's Wrong with This Picture," *Moving Out*, 1986
"Natural Attractant," *Soundings East*, 1986
"Decubitus," *Dan River Press*, 1986
"Mutuality," *American Short Fiction*, 1997
"Radiance of Matter" (the last section of "We're All in This Together"), *Passages North*, 1989
"Vanishing: 1965," *Fugue*, 2007

Library of Congress Cataloging-in-Publication Data

Lawrence, Candida.
Vanishing / Candida Lawrence.
p. cm.
ISBN 978-1-932961-66-9
Includes bibliographical references.
I. Title.
AC8.L3735 2009
818'.603—dc22
2008056056

1 3 5 7 9 10 8 6 4 2

Book Design by SH • CV

First Printing

TABLE OF CONTENTS

1942   *Everything She Does, and Says, and Is*   *3*

1965   *What's Wrong with This Picture?*   *15*

1965   *Vanishing: 1965*   *41*

1968   *Getting There*   *59*

1968   *Mom Wants to Write*   *69*

1970   *Mitterrand's Last Supper*   *83*

1970   *Sartorial Notes on a Man I Knew Once
       upon a Time, May He Rest in Peace*   *91*

1980   *Comforter*   *97*

1981   *We're All in This Together: A Memoir*   107

1982   *Natural Attractant*   183

1982   *My Past Tense*   195

1984   *Based on Experience*   207

1990   *Mutuality*   219

1993   *What Raymond Carver and I Talk*
       About . . .   231

1996   *Pacific Heights*   241

2006   *. . . Gone, All Gone*   247

2007   *I'm in a State*   261

Vanishing

Everything She Does, and Says, and Is

My sister Anne wanted to explain a few things.
She said: "I'll tell the story of long ago."
She asked me to take dictation, over a few days.
When she read my transcript she said:
"So, that's it, so true, all of it."

I'm sitting at my desk in the *Daily Cal* office. I have all my *private* papers here in a drawer I can lock with a key I keep on a string around my neck. There's now nothing at home for my pesky sister to snoop into—or my mother or father, though I don't believe they snoop. I'm in my second year as girl-who-does-everything, including writing this or that, and my position here is thrilling, *infinitely* more exciting than my course work. I can lie to my parents about what I'm doing, where I am (though I usually try to tell them the truth). I can lie because I'm working on a newspaper!

It's now seven-thirty and I just returned from 'Til Two, the bar down Telegraph Avenue, where I joined some staffers for a game of bridge and lots of good talk and a few beers. I'm guzzling ginger ale in hopes that the beer breath will evaporate before I get a ride home with the Editor, whenever he decides to leave. He lives off-campus in an apartment and can stay out all night if he wishes.

The *problem* is that the damn Administration has caught up with me and has ordered me to complete English 1A, which I've been dodging for almost two years. I took the first half of the one-year course and then just slipped away. It was so stupid, all those freshmen writing asinine papers, the girls in their great clothes and perfect bodies, the few boys (because we're at war) looking so 4F in their ROTC uniforms. All the girls except me were in sororities and that made me feel bad though I tried to rustle up some pride and not care that I didn't even get rushed so I could pretend I was not humiliated by being turned down. This is a mystery. I'm intelligent, from good family, not bad-looking, but it's as though I have some awful odor which makes these in-girls avoid me. Not that I'd join if asked. I'm against sororities; they are politically absurd. But I'd like to be asked, then refuse.

The *assignment*, due in two days: Write 1,000 words on a member of your family—your father, your mother, your sister, your brother. When the TA said "1,000 words" there were gasps of panic in the room. These students can burble on endlessly about nothing, but a thousand words on paper sounded to them like high literature. We've known about this task for weeks, and therefore I've had much time to think. I know what is expected—a *Reader's Digest* saccharine ode to a member of one's family. (The *Reader's Digest* is the *only* periodical not allowed in our house. No one reads it and yet we all know what kind of article it just *loves*.) The trouble for me is that I'm in a phase of my life when I dislike every member of my family, except our cocker spaniel and KitKat. My sister snoops, as I said, and raids my closet for items she wants to wear, then lies when confronted by proof. My little brother is a brat, holds his breath until he turns blue when denied something he wants. My mother says things like, "Why have you dyed your hair blonde when your brown color was so nice?" and "Have you put on a little bit of weight lately?" and "Purple lipstick? . . . maybe just a touch of old rose would go better with your complexion," and worst of all, "Isn't your beige sweater a bit boxier, not so tight?" Fact is, she hates my body. She doesn't want me to attract anyone with my bosom, which is substantial; she wants boys to like me for my intelligence. (She wears corsets, even when she gardens, and support hose, Red Cross brown oxfords.)

As for my father, by far the most interesting subject for an essay, he doesn't know it but I've been compiling a dossier on him for years, which is easy to do because he's a San Francisco daily columnist, syndicated across the country in 250 newspapers, and he sometimes writes about *me*, his daughter, which is unforgivable. He never asks permission, and for as long as I can remember I've had to go to school and have people I don't even know come up to me and say: "Oh, I read about you in yesterday's paper," and I'd say: "No, that wasn't me, that was my sister," and then, "It sounded like you; it was a sweet article." Yeah, sweet, which he is not.

I have a collection of his articles, those about me and others, offensive politically and/or morally, in my locked desk drawer. I'd been carrying them with me, in a binder, for years, which might lead one to believe that I admire them. One night, down at 'Til Two, they fell out onto the table and before I could grab them up, they were read (with cynical laughter, groans) and I felt for the first time understood. They said: "What a charlatan!" "What mush!" "What is he *really* like? Get this: 'He (the father) hopes she does not see this article. It is not the best thing for a little girl to know that her father and mother watch everything she does and says AND IS.' Who elected him God?" That night I disburdened myself and locked them in a drawer.

I feel as though I'm working on the Assignment, but deviously. I know I'll report only my admiration for my father, which is there, buried beneath a consuming dislike. (If I even *started* a critique of him, for public view, I would dissolve, cry.) After all, he's a successful writer and that's what I want to be. He was amazingly successful right here at this university—a scholarship student, on the *Occident* staff, the *Blue & Gold*, writer of Senior Extravaganza (text and lyrics and actor in black-face), editor of the *Pelican*, the campus humor magazine. All this from a fatherless poor boy from Watsonville High. He was a pacifist, joined the Ambulance Corps and served in France, was gassed and got the Croix de Guerre (his hair turned white). No floundering time. He was instantly a writer for the *San Francisco Call Bulletin* and he churns out articles faster than I can decide to go to my Underwood portable and *try* to write. (I have heard that typewriter ribbons are going to be scarce during this war and that no typewriters will be manufactured. I must go buy ribbons for what is now called The Duration.)

He is always watching. Last Saturday night I had a date, went to a movie, then parked a while with my date on the street near our gate. When he walked me to the front door, and I turned to kiss him goodnight, suddenly my father was there (at two a.m.) yelling, "WHERE HAVE YOU BEEN? WHAT HAVE YOU BEEN DOING? WHORE!" My date fled, I burst into tears and ran upstairs to my room. I could almost see dirt all over my arms, my pink angora sweater. I could hear his feet coming up the stairs, hesitate, then move on to his bedroom. I heard my sister say "WHAT is going ON?" then her door closing, my mother sobbing, "How *could* you?" said to my father.

Although his behavior with me is, at times, inexcusable and just plain nuts and causes me to wilt and want to die, I recover the instant I walk into my office on campus. My date does not exist here. He was merely a stray soldier from somewhere back east I met at a dance given locally for lonely servicemen. My profound quarrel with my father is more elevated and dates from many years back. I have been tracking the chasm between his public popularity, the acclaim he receives from his soggy readers, the *person* he projects with his writing—all that—and the sullen, witty, satirical, mean, brooding father I know at home. I have never let him know my contempt for his duplicity, and he certainly doesn't know that I carry around the offending articles. I'm waiting until my knowledge of the world catches up to my private disgust. Not now, not in an assignment for English 1A.

My stealthy pursuit of his corruption began when I was nine. I had been in an explosion in our neighborhood. I was burned, my face, my hands, and shards of glass were embedded in my chest and arms. I was at home, not yet allowed to go back to school, my hair growing back, my burns were not too serious, and the deepest wound in my chest was bandaged and healing. There was nothing for me to do but read and rest and play with KitKat. One afternoon, my friend Peggy was with me. Her hand burns were more serious, but we'd been having fun cutting out paper dolls that she herself had drawn on stiff white paper. My mother opened my bedroom door and held out to us the *San Francisco Call Bulletin*. "Your father wrote an article about you. You might like to read it."

The article was titled "A Little Girl Who Threatened to 'Leave Home.'" The first part describes (accurately) a goodbye note I wrote one day. "I have left this house forever! I will not stand another day with a cross mother and a pestering sister. Goodby!!!" He calls me "the young woman" and he says I went back to brush my teeth and then was off to school. He continues:

And that afternoon this young woman of 9 nearly did leave home forever. She went to a fire. She wasn't supposed to go, but other little girls were going, and why shouldn't she? So she went, and a terrible thing happened. There was an explosion, and dozens of them were injured. Streaming blood from wounds in her face, fearfully burned, she was taken to a hospital by a stranger, and it was an hour before her anxious family found her. . . . There she lay on a table, moaning a little, but otherwise quiet—a pathetic, heartbreaking mess. If she had cut her finger at home she would have yelled bloody murder, but here, badly injured, she wasn't howling, she wasn't clamoring for attention; she was waiting her turn patiently, and it was even said that she had told a doctor to fix up another little girl first, because SHE could wait. She was being a good sport, and through all the agony of the following days and nights she continued to be a good sport. The same little girl who had threatened to leave home forever, during that emergency acted like the young woman she had imagined she was.

All the other little girls and the other little boys were just as brave . . . showed those same qualities of sturdy courage . . . it makes me ashamed of adults. It lifts me up a little, gives me more power, makes me stronger. Doesn't it do that to you?

Peggy read the article over my shoulder and then lovingly touched it with her bandaged hand and kissed it. She said: "Please thank your father for me," and I said I would and held my resentment inside. Even now, ten years later, when I am nineteen, I find it hard to discover the entry hole where I can mount my attack. Let me try:

First, the day I "threatened to leave home forever" occurred at least a year before the explosion.

Second, what am I, a young woman or a "little girl"?

Third, he knows now, and knew when he wrote the article, that I was not being a "good sport" but was feeling a terrible guilt because not only had I gone to a fire when I'd promised my mother that very day that I wouldn't, I also had lied to everyone who questioned me. Question: Where were you when the house blew up? Answer: I was not in front of the house, I was *across the street!* I held onto this lie until put on the witness stand during the lawsuit against Pacific Gas & Electric, when I broke down, sobbed the truth, and was helped to my seat beside my parents.

Fourth, he knows I won't challenge him, didn't then, won't now. He came in free, in a newspaper, a place where I fervently believe truth must live, with fiction about a real daughter. He did this for the idiot readers who adore him.

Fifth, "leave home forever" is a metaphor for death worth seven loud groans.

I'm a sophomore, and maybe it's sophomoric to demand that writing about real events cleave to the truth. I know that my friends here at the *Daily Cal* are larnin' me about the sin of sentimentality, and the code we all follow which dictates that we cut out "marshmallow," hunt down the facts, believe nothing until we've checked and checked.

But let's look at marshmallow and fathers spying on daughters. This is what he wrote in an article entitled "Little Girl into Woman."

> I happen to know a little girl who went to see Katharine Hepburn in "Little Women" and she hasn't been the same since. Sometimes she stands before the fireplace and lets her dress billow out, just as Katharine did. She puts her hands behind her back, just as Jo wasn't supposed to do. She walks across the room with a characteristic Hepburn stride. And one evening for probably the first time in her life, she declined a piece of cake, with the idea, perhaps, of being as slender as that actress some day. . . . And a father looking at her closely can almost see that Katharine Hepburn moving in and out of his small daughter. Tomorrow, perhaps, she may be a little girl again, but she may not be.

She may, while his eyes were elsewhere, have made that magical, irrevocable change from girlhood into womanhood and no one may ever see that little girl again. He can't tell about that. It is one of those uncertainties that make parenthood interesting.

Now isn't that charming? Who could object? I can't stop his writing, indeed it pays the bills. And he does write well, doesn't he? (except for all those *hoods*). But I don't want him *ever* to watch me, write about me, analyze me for his public. There should be a law.

His worst sin is more recent, occurring about a year ago when Son, my beloved cousin, died in an Air Force accident. He burned up *inside* a plane *on the ground* and the government said oops, oh so sorry. There was a funeral attended by hundreds of weeping Santa Clara residents, all ages, who had known him all his life. I thought I would cry forever. He was my first kiss, in his barn where there was soft hay. Just kisses and the good smell of hay and horses and dog.

My father's long obituary column about Son and his funeral was featured on the front page and was titled "An American Boy Comes Home." The casket (containing ashes?), the folded flag given to his weeping mother, the gun salute. I clutched my stomach, made a fist, and didn't speak to him for a week, during which many people called to thank him for his "beautiful" words. My pacifist father said: "Yes, (the flag) was all she had left, except for a forever enduring pride in the strength and courage of the man she had given to her country . . . the mothers, too, are brave. And their sons, at last, come home to them."

What I learned: "come home" and "leave home" both mean death.

IT'S PAST MIDNIGHT, the Editor wants to go home. I've cleared some of the fog from my head and have just about decided to write about KitKat for English 1A.

What's Wrong with This Picture?

Saturday, May 15, 1965. At seven a.m. Jack and I board a plane for San Diego. We sit side-by-side and stare out the window at ships and sailboats. Jack reads the morning newspaper and after the Sports section, he adjusts his seat for maximum recline, takes my hand into his lap, and falls asleep. He can sleep anywhere, in any position. He has $500 and a telephone number in his pocket. I sit beside him, dry-eyed and neutral.

I feel his hand grow lax. I turn away from watching clouds and stare at him. His massive head is half-buried in an airline pillow, the hair frizzes out dark on the white linen and the tufted eyebrows form a ledge over the dusky, worried skin of his eyelids. All of his force seems jammed up behind eyes and twitching full lips, half open, hissing now and then.

Beneath my cotton skirt I feel this man's warm liquid seep downward, the residue of "one more time before . . . ," a last homogenizing before the separation of showers, shaving, wheels, highways, buckled seatbelts.

Jack opens his eyes. I have often noticed that he cannot sleep if I have a worried mind, even though my body remains as still as a flat snake on the road. He sits up and punches the button on his armrest. The chair back jumps forward and the pillow falls to the floor. He glances at his watch. We move together to retrieve the pillow and bump heads. Jack groans and we laugh.

"Madam," he says softly, "we're going to land in a few minutes. We can place a call when we land, or we can rent a car and take a short trip across the border, laze around, and reverse our steps, and *not* telephone. Or we can telephone, rent a car, and stay in San Diego overnight, and return home tomorrow morning, without crossing the border. We can stay in the airport and book the first flight home. If you're muddled . . . if you don't wish to . . . just give me a sign. It's all right . . . whatever *you* decide."

He is speaking into my ear and his warm breath makes my throat ache with tears I will not shed. I kiss his cheek and turn away to stare at all the kidney-shaped spots of blue growing larger as the plane banks and seems to drift downward towards reunion with others of its own kind.

"This is your pilot Eliot Carter. We'll be landing at San Diego Airport in about five minutes. The temperature at ground level is a fine 65 degrees and it's another beautiful day for the San Diegans. We thank you for flying United."

I turn towards Jack, who is making no effort to join the line of passengers crowding the aisle.

"Let's call," I say into his ear. "Let's act as if and postpone shall or shall not for a little while. My body wants to feel good again and in San Diego a tragic view of life is unseemly . . . perhaps even against the law." I wish I could hug or kiss him, but he doesn't like a public display of affection. We join the line of people filing slowly towards the exit door, Jack in front of me, my hot cheek pressing against his cool blue nylon shoulder.

Jack parks me in a café booth next door to a gas station telephone kiosk. I can look out the window and watch him search his pockets for change and notepaper. He plucks a pen from the row of implements he wears clipped to his shirt pocket. He dials a number and turns back, and with his free hand closes the folding door behind him. A waitress with dyed blond hair in a net sets a glass of water in front of me.

"There'll be two of us. We'll order when he returns." I try a smile. I wonder if another woman once sat here, on another day, waited while her male companion telephoned, and said to the same waitress . . . "There'll be two of us . . ." I want to ask her: "Have you had an abortion across the border?" I suddenly want to know about other women, to sit on comfortable pillows in a large wood-paneled interior, listening to voices of testimony, proud or ashamed. I would console the women, wipe away their tears with pretty hankies, hold tightly in my arms a hiccupping, sodden abandonee, be wise and soothing. The waitress moves away to take an order at the next table. I wonder what a woman would do without a Jack. Are there solitary women who make the trip from Nebraska or Missouri, who hitchhike to save borrowed or stolen cash, call a number, catch a bus into a foreign land? *Is* there a bus? Do they come with a mother or sister or friend, or perhaps even a husband . . . a father? No, no father. If Jack had refused, would I have come alone? No. I am not afraid of spiders, strange men, living alone—but I could not have traveled across a border into a loss of language and consciousness, into a blood-spurt with cold instruments inserted by a stranger's trembling fingers—without Jack. I would have squatted in inertia's puddle. Or would I?

I watch Jack open the folding door and walk casually towards a row of newspaper-vending machines. He searches his pocket for a dime, inserts it in a slot, and places the *L.A. Times* under one arm. He glances back over his shoulder as he walks towards the café. I grab my purse and walk swiftly in the direction of a glittering, pink Rest Room sign. I will wash my face, comb my hair, smooth my rumpled skirt, and try to look my prettiest for the best of all possible guides. We both like as-if games. We shall pretend to be tourists with an unusual stop marked on our itinerary.

WE RENT A 1965 FORD SEDAN, blue with a white interior, AM-FM radio, and a clock that works. I sit primly on the dazzling vinyl and feel small. Jack turns on the radio and tunes the red marker to Joan Baez singing "Lord Randal." He pulls his cap over one eye and asks: "Where to, Madam?"

"To Mexico! When and where are we to go?" I try for a light tone.

"Eleven-fifteen at the Woolworth parking lot."

"Then what?"

"We're to meet a white station wagon. Someone will drive us to the Cliníque."

"Us? Are you sure they'll let you go?"

"I'm certainly going to try to go wherever they take you." He hands his driver's license to a man who stands stiff and tall in front of a tiny office. He returns the card between two fingers, leans down to peer into the car, and waves us on. The wide street with insurance offices, travel agencies, motels and cafés lining both sides, narrows abruptly as we move slowly forward behind a caravan of tourists. Behind us, a pickup truck containing brown laughing children is waved to the side. A man in uniform talks with the driver—a brown face chewing insolently on a toothpick, under a broad-brimmed hat. The children in the back of the truck sit very still, smiling, their teeth glittering in the sunlight.

Jack drives faster now, and I face front, my hands in my lap. We bump across a railroad track, and a sign at the side of the road says "TIJUANA 5 MILES," but already the narrow road is filled with brown bodies criss-crossing, ambling, running, laughing, thumping the trunk of the car with mocking good humor. I had expected color, but everywhere I look the monotonous brown of old paint, dried weeds, dust, and mud-flecked cars reflects upwards until even the blue sky of the United States yields, fused with a beige light, like a vast tent dome, staked at ground level by alleys and tilted wooden small buildings.

"Do you want to get out and wander around? We have time." Jack reaches for my hand. I let him lift it, squeeze, and return it to my lap.

"No." This is the first time the flat no-trespass negative has come naturally to my lips. It feels fine, like a new garment that fits just so, but evokes no comment. I fold my hands and stare straight ahead, seeing nothing. I am hidden, sealed in self, and Jack doesn't matter. He is a car-part, pushing a right foot down, turning a wheel, aiming, pulling a round knob, lifting a leg. The car will find the way to the Woolworth parking lot. There is no reason to concern myself. I can concentrate on pricking him with spiked silence, stabbing his composure by removing his companion. I can refuse to play "as-if," or "we might as well enjoy ourselves on the way to . . . ," and especially "We're in this together." I'll be satisfied if he starts bleeding through the heart of his blue gingham shirt and tears ooze from blinking eyes.

He drives slowly, trying to discover a street sign. "Have you seen what street we're on? Christ! This traffic! Did you see that guy? He nearly hit that old lady!"

I don't answer. The road widens and we leave behind the tattered display of sidewalk markets and tourists, the crush of barefoot children hanging onto their mamas' sagging skirts, voices pitched high, shouting over the blat of Elvis, Chuck Berry, and Mexican rock-and-roll erupting from dark doorways. On both sides of the straight highway, sere, uncultivated land matches and meets a beige sky. Here and there a crumpled house in the distance, a wrecked car, a tire in a ditch, a fan belt on the road, a flattened snake. Suddenly, a second city emerges; motels, gas stations, cafés, a lone tall building in the distance, taxicabs, modern storefronts, banks, pawnshops, more tourists, street signs. Jack slows down at a four-way electric green, red, and yellow stoplight. He stretches his neck to see the street sign, then spins left, cars honking at him from the rear. He drives two blocks, turns right, and I see the familiar red and gold Woolworth storefront, just like Durant, Wyoming, or Berkeley, but larger, occupying almost half a block.

Jack drives around the corner to the parking lot entrance. He approaches slowly and rides the slight incline as though the car is made of fine glass and he carries a bomb in the seat next to him. The white station wagon is parked against the rear wall of Woolworth's, and although the lot is filled with automobiles of every size and color, my eyes fuse to white metal.

The clock on the dash reads 11:05 and in ten minutes something is going to happen. I pull my thighs and knees safely in against my chest until the pressure hurts. I can view the parking lot through the rear window, and I remember a booklet one used to be able to buy at Woolworth's: "What Is Wrong with This Picture?" The drawing on page one was always easy—perhaps the rabbit had a long tail or the rooster had whiskers—and when I had circled the erroneous item, I could turn to page two, which contained more errors embedded in a more intricate drawing. The parking lot picture has errors that I want to fix. Jack and I are looking out the rear window and although we are uncomfortably warm, our windows are shut. Three women are sitting on side benches in the station wagon. They look bloodless and still, like statues, but staring from shining eyes. A well-dressed black woman stands in the middle of the parking lot. She watches the bench-sitters and flicks ash onto the ground. Ten feet from her, a man and a woman, not young and dressed like American tourists, press against each other. The woman's stiff hair tilts against his chest. He wears a gold wedding band and over her shoulder, he watches the white wagon. A Mexican, smoking a brown cigarette, lounges against the side of the wagon. Around his elbow, he wears a glittering gold watch with expansion wristband. Between nervous puffs, he raises his arm to check the time. No one is talking. Everyone in the parking lot stands or sits in the wagon's magnetic field. The Mexican is in charge. That too seems wrong.

Suddenly he flips his cigarette over the fence and opens the door on the driver's side. He leans on the open door and stares blankly at the parking lot. Jack gets out of the car and walks quickly towards the station wagon. The man with the golden wedding ring follows. The men huddle, heads bent towards the ground. I leave the car, and as I walk towards Jack, I hear: "No—no-no, por favor, señores, hombres . . . no . . . solamente las mujeres . . . solamente . . . sí, sí . . . one hour y . . . a la una." He holds out his watch and points. "Aquí . . . comprenden ustedes? . . . sí . . . O.K.?"

The men break huddle. The Mexican climbs into the driver's seat and punches the horn lightly, twice. Jack walks towards me. He stops two feet in front of me. "No men allowed. He'll return at one o'clock. Sweetheart . . ."

"Where's the money?"

He pulls his wallet from his pocket and hands me five $100 bills. I stuff them loosely in my purse and turn to walk towards the wagon. He steps in front of me and pulls my stiff body into his arms. He lifts my face with a gentle finger and kisses dry, closed lips. I wait for him to release me and, without looking at him, walk to the white wagon, open the door, and seat myself beside the black woman. The woman with the hairdo climbs in and sits down facing me. There are tears in her eyes. I sit up straight, my knees locked tightly together, and look out at the two men standing beside their cars, waving goodbye. The driver backs up, nudges a garbage can, then drives swiftly to the exit.

Jack raises a hand, places it on his lips, raises it again. My eyes blur and I try to make my arm move up. Too late. I turn my head and try to smile. My lips are like dried paper glued on the front of my head. The wagon moves into traffic at a brisk speed and I have to hang onto the seat to keep my body from falling into the lap across from me or scrunching the bodies next to me. Already I am sorry and now I have to stay alive so that I can return to that tiny figure beside a blue Ford and tell him so.

I cling to the seat as the wagon cuts through alleys, around corners, one block left, then right, finally circling back to a wider road into the country. I try to remember the route from the parking lot and think of Hansel, or was it Gretel, dropping crumbs onto the forest path. The driver shifts his eyes from rear-view mirror to road and back again, and I know he is not watching his passengers. For the first time, I realize that he is afraid, and that this journey in a wagon filled with silent women is as dangerous for him as crossing enemy lines in a white jeep in the moonlight. His fear leaks to the rear and I hope we soon find cover.

The driver now settles into his seat and lights a cigarette. He is much younger than he appeared to be in the parking lot, and as he sits hunched over the wheel, he might be any teenager allowed to drive the family car into the country, testing its power, watching for the highway patrol, six ghostly mothers in the rear, insubstantial reminders of traffic laws he has forgotten as soon as he put key into ignition.

Six silent women taking a ride with a brown teenager in an American station wagon on a country road in Mexico. What is wrong with this picture? I inspect the passengers. Each sits with knees locked, eyes fixed on a point somewhere past the woman who faces her, an identical posture.

To my right is Black Woman, calm, dignified. Next to Black Woman is a young girl, certainly not more than nineteen. She is dressed in faded jeans, with a gray-white man's shirt covering her stomach. Her hair is dirty-blond in both color and texture, the face mush-colored with bruised pimples for decoration. Her eyes are red from recent weeping and seem about to spill over again. Facing Young Girl on the bench opposite, is an older woman in a light-blue pants suit. Her hands are folded over a black patent leather satchel that matches sandals peeking, twinkling, on tiny stockinged feet. I would have guessed her to be too old for this trip, but perhaps she has similar thoughts about me. There is humor in her eyes, and suppressed conviviality in the patterns she is tapping out on her handbag. Next to Blue-Pants-Suit sits an elegant female in mid-twenties, dressed in bright pink madras folds down to her slender ankles. Beneath the madras, long slender arms with gold bangles are sheathed in a black leotard, and around her neck golden chains sparkle in the sunlight. Her black hair is long and she wears it loosely tied back with a narrow satin cord ending in a tiny brass bell. She must be the source of the incense smell that masters all rivals in our enclosure. Her bag dangles beads and feathers, and the face, which looks out from the soft dark hair, is serene. Her feet, in toe-hold leather sandals, are crossed at the ankles. The last passenger, seated next to Patchouli-Madras, is the weeping housewife with the hairdo who found it so difficult to part from her loving husband in the parking lot. Or is he perhaps someone else's loving husband? I wish I could ask.

Trying to catch an eye is like trying to fish with no bait. While I watch the road I can feel Patchouli-Madras's eyes travel over me, but when I slowly turn my head towards the smooth shoulders, her eyes glide into a space just past my right ear. I remember reading that Jews packed into boxcars maintained a silence, which irritated their captors, maddened them into gratuitous, frenzied cruelty, which produced communal chants, but a single voice did not speak out to a neighbor, and no one uttered a sound to a being on the other side of pain. Are we captives? If so, who has captured us? If we could sing, what song would it be? "Where Have All the Babies Gone"? "Take Me Back to Tulsa, I'm Too Young to Miscarry"? "Nearer My God to Thee"? Why can't I speak to them? I want to. I need to—but I can't talk of detergents, TV, boyfriends, husbands, lovers . . . or babies. We're not sick. I can't speak of illness.

The wagon swerves suddenly to the right shoulder and then turns left, speeding up a dirt road lined with decaying cypress. The wheels spin in a clayey dust and we hold onto the wooden benches, squinting ahead at what appears to be a slight rise in the desolate, dry land. Black crows dip their wings at the noisy intrusion. The engine whines in first gear, the trees disappear, then a steep descent to a bare white stucco wall. The brakes scream and a door lifts slowly. We drive inside the wall to a white courtyard and park against the side of a small ranch house. I look behind me at our entry point and see a wall without an opening. I want to laugh. What webs we weave. Man should be called spider, and spider something else.

The driver slides from his seat and waves his arm at a door marked ENTRADA. He slips through another door and disappears. Black Woman climbs out first and I follow her. Inside, after the white brilliance, there is little to be seen. Dark hallways with closed doors. A female attendant silently leads us to a room and stands guard until six women have arranged themselves on two small couches and four chairs.

"Wait please," she says and closes the door. A young woman is lying on the couch, a pillow clutched across her stomach. She is crying and moaning. Black Woman, Patchouli-Madras, Housewife and I sit in chairs. Blue-Pants-Suit sits on a couch. Young Girl squeezes herself onto the couch with the pillow-clutcher, her eyes staring at the disheveled hair, the swollen cheeks. Slim fingers knead a wrinkled pillowcase.

Blue-Pants-Suit settles her patent leather bag beside her on the couch. She crosses her legs and runs her fingers over dusty sandals. She gazes at the girl and speaks kindly: "Have you had . . . are you waiting? . . . what hurts?"

"Everything hurts! They won't let me go home. They say I have to wait until the next wagon goes . . . they say I'm crying too much. I want to go!" She pushes her face into the pillow.

"Now-now, you'll feel better soon. You're just frightened." She turns to Young Girl. "Change places with me, will you?" She sits down next to the wet face. "Come now—put your head in my lap and I'll try some of my famous massage. It always makes you feel better!"

Pillow-Clutcher lets her pillow be arranged in the blue lap and shifts to her back, her head resting comfortably, her feet draped over the arm of the couch. Blue-Pants-Suit removes two diamond rings, one from each hand, and sets them inside the girl's left hand, closing the fingers gently. She places a hand on each temple and begins to rub back and forth, her fingers pushing rhythmically.

"Now, doesn't that feel better?"

No answer. The girl closes her eyes.

"Why do you say it hurts? It's not supposed to hurt." Young Girl asks the question and looks around the room for an answer.

"They lied. It *does* hurt, and it hurt when they did it. They didn't put me out. They tried to . . . but I felt the *whole* thing!" She rubs her stomach with fists and then opens her hand to look at the rings.

"I don't think it helps much to have her going on that way . . ." Housewife looks to me for agreement.

"Maybe it helps her to talk about it . . . and maybe she was further along than . . ." My voice sounds thin and wispy. I clear my throat.

"I'm ten weeks," Blue-Pants-Suit volunteers.

"I'm six weeks," Housewife says firmly.

Patchouli-Madras stares at her hands.

Black Woman says: "I pass."

"I'm six weeks," I offer, pleased with this round-robin.

"But *I'm* three months! . . . I think . . ." Young Girl gasps.

"And you, little sufferer? Your turn." Blue-Pants-Suit is working now on the girl's shoulders and neck.

"Three and a half months!" I think I detect pride in the announcement. ". . . and it cost me $800 . . . and it hurt!"

"They told me $600—I wonder why the difference." Housewife, a consumer's inquiry. Round-robin again.

"Same here," says Blue-Pants-Suit. We ignore Patchouli-Madras and move on to Black Woman. She smiles at us and passes, but less firmly than before.

"$500," I announce.

"$750 for me . . . it must be how far along you are." Young Girl struggles with this thought.

The attendant opens the door and nods to Black Woman. She stands up quickly and follows the attendant; the door closes behind her. Silence. A few moans, softer now.

"I wish she hadn't passed. Maybe she didn't want to talk 'cause she's black. Me, I feel lots better when I talk. My son says I talk too much." We watch Blue-Pants-Suit, hoping she'll go right on talking. "He's twenty-five years old an' he still lives with me . . . but he has his own life, an' I have mine. It was falling down the cellar stairs that did it . . . it jiggled everything somehow . . . an' when my monthly didn't come, at first I thought I was just skipping because of the fall . . . too early for menopause. Was I surprised when the doctor told me! I've got a good man, but he's got grown kids, an' we're fine the way we are. We don't want a new family. We don't even want to get married! Hope I'm not shockin' anyone. It'd be nice . . . to have a baby . . . but I've got a job I like . . . an' you know . . . I don't think it's fair to the baby." She looks around the room for support. Housewife leans forward stiffly.

"My husband thinks—we think that three children is all we can afford. They're teenagers and we want them to go to college. We thought about it for a long time. Well, not so long, but it seemed long. In Nebraska, where we live . . . well . . . our doctor told us about this place, and . . . Afterwards, we're going to spend our vacation in Los Angeles and see Disneyland. We've never been . . ." She pulls a pink hankie from her purse and dabs her nose and eyes.

The door opens. The attendant dips her head to Patchouli-Madras. She gathers together her colorful draped elegance, and with a graceful nod to Housewife and me, she lifts her head high and departs. The door closes.

"Christeroo! That's a cool number. What perfume was she wearing? Like she was here but not here. That's the way we all feel

I guess . . . but she was kinda snooty. Oh . . . I dunno. Maybe she can't speak English or is shy. What do I know? I shouldn't knock her. I have a feelin' I'm next. I get these feelings an' my man is amazed, I'm usually right. My son . . . he gets mad at me when I go on about the feelings. Says it's just the odds or common sense, but it's not. Here I am talking again. My son . . . he says . . . but I guess I told you that . . . about talking too much. My man likes it, says it saves him thinkin' what to say."

"Do you want me to take over the massage now?" My words fall from my mouth. Pillow-Clutcher opens her eyes to see who has volunteered. She lifts her head and pulls her knees up to her stomach.

"That okay with you? You feel a bit better now?" Blue-Pants-Suit stands up and stretches her arms above her head, smooths her mussed lap, and trades places with me. I sit down. The girl puts her pillow in my lap and lies down on her stomach with her head in the pillow. I hesitate, then place my stiff, cool fingers on the girl's shoulders.

"Sorry about the cold. My hands'll be warm in a few minutes. Just relax. That's better." It feels good to be touching warm skin, to be helping, doing, moving in rhythm, to talk, to listen.

"God! I'm gonna fix my face. If I'm next, I want to look good. I always say that wherever you go you should look your best. I won't even answer the phone in the morning 'til my face is on. My man, he laughs at me. He thinks I look good even before I get out of bed. But he's prejudiced. Here . . . hold this for me, will ya?" Blue-Pants-Suit sits down on the couch next to Young Girl and hands her a small looking glass with a rhinestone-studded handle. Young Girl uses two hands to hold the mirror; her fingernails are bitten and torn almost down to the first knuckle.

"Your folks waitin' for you in San Diego?" Blue-Pants-Suit tugs at an eyelash which displeases her.

"My folks? No . . . I mean . . . my mother an' my boyfrien' will pick me up. My dad is so mad . . . we dint even tell him Johnny was coming. He's jes' *so* mad, he won't even let him in the house or talk to him or *anything* . . . but we're gonna get married as soon as Johnny gets a job . . . an' he's gonna pay Mom back all the money. We love each other . . . we really do . . . we never had no one else . . . an' Dad hit me an' he won't talk to me either . . . we dint mean to go the limit . . . it was an accident . . . we thought . . ."

"Hold that mirror steady! Now don't go makin' things worse by cryin'! Here, use my comb . . . you look drowned out . . . you're gonna scare the nurse, if there is a nurse. You're lucky to have a nice Johnny waitin' for you. I'm sure he's a good boy."

The attendant opens the door and nods to Blue-Pants-Suit.

"See? What'd I tell you! If I thought he'd listen I'd tell my son it worked again!" She snaps her purse shut and stands up. She performs a brisk Shirley Temple tap-routine, and groans loudly. She salutes Pillow-Clutcher and flicks her heel up to her bottom as she goes past the couch. As the door closes, we hear her say: "Well, here goes nuthin!"

I rub, and the girl seems to be sleeping. One hand holds the gaudy rings, but loosely now, as though the hand is giving up responsibility for a last detail of living. I place my finger on the girl's pulse . . . one . . . two . . . three . . . four . . . a steady push against fragile skin. Young Girl curls herself into her boyfriend's shirt with her dirty feet tucked up under her. She rubs her wet nose on one faded blue knee. Her hair sticks together like pulled taffy.

I wonder if all the rooms are sound-proofed. Even when the door is open, there is no hint of human existence beyond the threshold. No squeak of swift nurses' feet, no computer voice on intercom, no creaking of gurney wheels, no wails or muffled groans, no sound of tires or engines entering or leaving the courtyard not more than twelve feet from where I sit. I have always loved the forest, or a bedroom at three in the morning and have called what I loved Silence. An interlude without human claim. No voices defining me. But this? What did Emily say? "Silence is all we dread. There's Ransom in a Voice!" She knew, Emily did, about Dread and waiting, and Loss, and a dying while yet living.

"This is the House of Lead—remembered, if outlived, as Freezing Persons, recollect the Snow—First—Chill—then Stupor—then Letting go." My hands move to the beat of capitalizations.

"What did you say? Did you say something to me?" The girl looks up at me, upside down, from my lap.

"Oh . . . I didn't realize I was speaking out loud. It was just a poem."

"It sounded sad . . . say it again."

"I don't think . . ."

"My father used to read poetry to me. He's dead. He read happy poems, and smiled and laughed when he read them. But later on, after he died . . . that's what my mother said . . . that he died . . . but I'm not sure . . . say the stuff about freezing persons."

I recite the poem from the beginning. The girl does not speak but seems to snuggle in closer to herself, as though wrapped in weightless blanket material. The attendant stands at the open door and nods to me.

"See you later—in the van," I say to my roommates, and follow the silent figure in white to a small desk in a corner of the hallway.

"The money, please."

I hand her $500. She turns a knob on top of a metal box which rests on the desk, lifts the latch, and lays the bills inside an empty interior, replaces the lid, and twirls the knob. She opens a door behind her and waits for me to enter a white room. "Take off everything below waist and wait. The doctor comes in a minute." She closes the door.

Chill. I see a high table covered with a white sheet. Metal cans with lids that go up and down when a foot presses, three of them, crouch against the wall. I remove my skirt and fold it neatly. There is no place to put the skirt, or my purse. I look at the linoleum floor, so speckled in pattern that I cannot determine its degree of cleanliness. I put my belongings in a corner. There are no windows, and I remember that the waiting room was windowless. I try to recall the exterior of the house, but I can't. I remove my shoes, pantyhose, and panties and place them carefully on top of my skirt.

I wait beside the white sheet. Three people enter the room, one of them a dark-brown man in a white jacket. Two women in white. Later, I cannot remember how I mounted or lay down on the table. There are brown hands, a sting in my buttock, and his eyes looking beyond my hips to the metal cans on the floor. When I can again see, a woman says: "Do not make noise. Lie quiet. I tell you when you can sit up." The woman is holding my wrist and looking at a watch. The voice speaks out to the walls and I cannot see her eyes.

"Por favor, please sit up. You have sanitary pad?" I push myself onto my elbows and nod. I feel quite dizzy. "Put it on. If room goes around, wait. Get dressed soon," she says over a starched shoulder as she is moving across the threshold. The door closes silently.

I sit up and dangle my legs over the side of the high table. I push off to the floor far below and my knees keep on going down.

I grab the side of the table. I crawl to the belt and sanitary pad in my purse and am surprised to find toilet paper stuffed into my vagina. I pull, and out comes a bright red wad. I push down the foot pedal with one hand and can see piles of red wads stacked almost to the top of the can. The underside of the lid is splashed with red. I adjust the belt and pad without standing up, pull on my panties, and decide not to wear my pantyhose because I don't trust my body to stay upright on one leg while I insert the other leg into a stocking, and so on. I don't want to lie down on the floor. I fasten my skirt and buckle my sandals. Sitting hurts a little, but far away, like a memory of pain.

By trial and error, I discover that I can achieve a standing posture by going the route of infancy—roll over to a crawl position, hang onto the table with one hand, one foot on the floor, pull, other hand on table, pull, put second foot on floor, pull up, push down, and I am there, able to rest across the white sheet, with two legs stretched out below a vacant numb area between thighs and waist. Now what? Dare I open the door? Am I supposed to wait? I stare at the metal can and wonder if what they took from me is still there, or has it been whisked to a nether incinerator which consumes the product of this factory? I open the door and walk slowly to the middle of the dark hallway. The pulse-taker approaches out of the shadows, her white uniform preceding the face.

"Instructions. Read and follow. This bottle has medicine. Take one pellet each four hours. Take one now." She hands me one pill, a sheet of paper with typed instructions, a container of capsules, and after I have placed the medicine on my tongue, magenta-tipped fingers offer a white paper cup. I take the cup and swallow a liquid that smells and tastes like chlorinated pool water.

A door opens and I step again into a room that may be the first room, but I can't be sure. One chair missing? Yes, that's it. And the colors—more gray, less brown.

"The wagon leaves in five minutes. Wait." The door closes. Black Woman, Patchouli-Madras, Blue-Pants-Suit, Housewife . . . is everyone present? Yes. No. Young Girl and Pillow-Clutcher are missing. I sit down carefully and close my eyes against the sight of four women who have become mannequins again. Each woman looks down, beyond, through, or over. They are awaiting release and concentrating, as I am, on someone standing in a parking lot, or leaning against a building in Tijuana, in a hotel room in San Diego, on a bus station bench in Santa Fe. Pants-Suit had said: "Here goes nuthin'!" and everyone knows you can't share or talk about "nuthin'." I have a "feelin'" eyes will find spaces between, and mouths will stay shut as we play our tape in reverse, out the door, into the van, through the magic wall-door, bumping down the road, hanging onto seats, speeding past beige wasted dry fields, swerving around corners, gliding into an unmarked space against the back wall of Woolworth parking lot, waiting politely for the mannequin in front to step onto oozing blacktop, and poof, be gone.

⬤　⬤　⬤

JACK IS BESIDE THE CAR, just where I left him, and I try to run. My legs wobble but my mouth works fine and I smile. He meets me halfway and the man who does not approve of a public display of affection starts at the top with a wet kiss and seals his body to mine. He buries his face in my neck. I bend my head and bite gently into blue nylon.

Vanishing: 1965

T he rules you must follow for a successful vanishing are few. They must be internalized and never forgotten:

PLAN AHEAD.

DO NOT EXPLAIN YOUR ACTIONS TO ANYONE, HOWEVER INNOCENT.

RECORD AND REMEMBER DOCUMENT FICTIONS.

DO NOT COMMUNICATE WITH FRIENDS OR RELATIVES BY U.S. MAIL OR TELEPHONE.

BOTH BEFORE AND AFTER, MAINTAIN APPEARANCE OF A CALM, LAW-ABIDING CITIZEN.

DO NOT REVEAL YOUR HISTORY TO NEW FRIENDS.

There have been instances when I have broken one or a combination of these rules and each time I have felt panic and loss of control. When I lost control, my body twitched and my nights filled with dreams of search, flight, prison. To calm myself, I smiled a lot. Occasionally I had to invent new fictions of surpassing pathos—an alcoholic mother—and then wait to discover the power of fiction.

One more rule: NEVER LIE TO THE CHILDREN. After you have vanished, they will hear you lie to others (birthdate, place of birth, explanations of father's whereabouts), but if they know the reasons for your lies they will know history and motive and can fit pieces into the puzzle. You are putting yourself in their power, but you've been there all along, haven't you?

To vanish. The word excites me. The idea is kin to reincarnation—to leave one realm and appear in another. Changing my hair color or facial features, or altering the looks of my children, even if possible, scarcely occurred to me. I knew I had an anonymous face, and time would swiftly change Louis and Emily. There was no blemish, scar, prominent mole on us that would cause anyone to take notice. No withered arm, wandering eye, or harelip. We were ordinary, and quickly would join the most unexamined group in America—women raising children alone. Our sole worrying distinction was that the children were smart, either as a result of the trouble they'd seen or natural endowment, but I could hardly tell them to dumb-down for a while. Both seemed to be born competitive, wanting to be first and best, to know the answers. With Louis, I gained six safe months by withholding him from kindergarten until he was willing to be called by his new name. Obligingly, he flunked his pre-Kg test and I was told he needed time to mature. When asked to count five dots he answered "green"; he said lemonade was "very, very orangey"; he listed three vehicles with wheels—"tricycles, cars, and ships." I didn't tell his interrogators that he'd been in one school or another since he was two, could speak passable Italian, had crossed the Atlantic in a ship, had shouted at a judge in full court: "You're mean! I want my mommy!" and that his greatest gift was comedy, displayed long before he had good reason to duck adult guidance. I did not explain to these authorities. An authority is anyone who has, or will have, power over you. Learn how to spot them.

In contrast to Louis, who wasn't ready to be a hero, Emily entered second grade as Linda Lawrence, answered to that name although she'd had it only two weeks, and kept a careful mouth. When I was a child, I admired Joan of Arc; when I was forty, I was awed and humbled by the bravery of my daughter, barely seven years old. Her solemn dignity made me seek mine, and yet I wondered in what direction the twig was being bent and whether a bonsai would grow in that place where I hoped for shimmering aspen.

To vanish. To pass suddenly from sight. Those left behind would not see me, they would receive no letters. No one could summon me to court, no warrant for my arrest could pass to my hand. Invisible children can't be taken from an invisible woman. In the second week, I walked barefoot beside the ocean, Louis lagging behind, squatting, poking a stick into seaweed pods, laughing at the pop, dragging a length of seaweed behind him, asking if he could take it home. We were tiny sculptures on sand. We walked up the lane into town. At a busy corner, inside a graffitied kiosk, I placed a call to my former school board chairwoman. Don't call again, the FBI has visited, your crime is now a felony, be well, be happy, we love you, don't call again, we don't like to lie. The dirty telephone booth and the anonymous gas station now seemed much too open, places where felons were watched. The cars, the gas pumps, the telephone had eyes. Louis, with his green and brown slimy sea-hair wrapped around his neck, was unmistakably "the boy," the woman was wearing Guilt. I was huge in my pink T-shirt, the white of my cutoffs dazzled, competed with the sun. I took his hand, he pulled it away. We walked home slowly, my feet wanting to run but awaiting my command.

Planning obsessed me while I waited for the children to be sent to me for their month-long, every-other-summer visit. Christmas, one week in alternate years. For the first time in my life I had a rel-atively long-range goal. By nature, I was a perverse non-planner, amazed by those women who not only knew what the family would be eating two weeks in the future but had already shopped for the ingredients and never ran out of toilet paper. If becoming a crimi-nal was my long-range goal, I knew I had to practice and this meant preparing my identity in advance. I needed to be sustained daily by a sense that I was ethical and was acting in the best interests of the children, but I couldn't find a source for sustenance. I had to look up at the moon and ask for help!

While you are waiting for the moon's advice, here's what you must do. Collect all the paper props of your existence: Social Security card, driver's license, birth certificate, school records, transcripts. Know that you'll be trashing all these items, but put all this paper in a pile and select a new name. This decision may take several days or even weeks, but don't rush. Your name, because chosen, must continue to encourage you through hard times ahead, but avoid a name that would cause anyone to ask questions. Talk to yourself: "Oh Mrs. Blank, could I trouble you to make a payment on your doctor's bill?" When the name feels warm, adventurous, perhaps even romantic but respectable, select a birthdate and birthplace. Name, birthdate, birthplace. Don't go exotic on birthplace. Choose a large metropolitan area like L.A. or New York. Select new birthdates for both yourself and your children. These birthdates should be as easy to remember as the real ones and should be in the same season of the year. Write all this on a piece of paper and memorize it. Then tear it up and stuff it at the bottom of someone else's garbage.

On a sunny day when you feel optimistic, drive at least fifty miles in any direction and post an application to the Social Security Administration with return address GENERAL DELIVERY at the post office in any nearby small town. If you're sure no one has followed you, present yourself at this town's motor vehicle office and start live lying. Say you're new in town and plan to stay but you don't have a driver's license, have never had one. Say your husband did all the driving but now you're divorced, gulp, and a cousin has been teaching you. In California, a photo is required. You can wear a kerchief and look down at your feet at the last moment. Refuse a fingerprint. It is optional. The clerk will not be pleased, but don't explain or apologize. Just say you'd rather not. You'll have to give the same address of GENERAL DELIVERY. The clerk won't like that either, but don't explain.

Birth certificates, college records, and transcripts are worthless but if you can't bear to part with them and are thinking you might learn forgery, bury them in the bottom of your suitcase. Amateur forgery is not a good idea; it can be detected by even the dullest of clerks. Professional forgery is expensive and risky, leading you into company you'd be wise to avoid.

Keep in focus whatever moral purpose you've been able to construct. And if this collapses, as it will, console yourself by remembering that you are at war, that the father has sole custody of the children, that he kidnaps them and maligns you, that you birthed them, that you've done no wrong except to leave him, that his quality time with his daughter is too intimate, that he has an evil temper, and that leaving will mean a cessation of these troubles and is in the best interests of the children.

All of this is old news and its litany now is to give you courage for surely the most desperate act of your life. When the voice inside your head bleats—"Oh, helpless lambs without a father!"—tell yourself that millions of children are without fathers and in any case, it's never been proved that a father is necessary for balanced growth and something called maturity, and there's much evidence to the contrary. None of this will ease your pain but is useful to carry you forward. You knew that action would be difficult, and while you're waiting to vanish, remember the torture of enforced passivity, the shameful role of a discarded mother, the children's empty beds, your feet that have nowhere to go, not even to Safeway to buy Wheaties and milk, the teaching position you lost because you couldn't be there and in court at the same time, the money you owe lawyers. Walk in maudlin shadow only long enough to stiffen your back.

If you have made your decision to vanish well in advance of actual possibility, as I did, you will have time to get strong before the children's summer or Christmas visit. Strength requires money and health. Fear will make your food back up, but clean the toilet and scrub it with Lysol. Try to re-gain the weight you've lost in court battles. I took on mindless survey and clerical jobs, and a summer Head Start classroom. I was, after all, a teacher, though much tattered. Still, a prepared teaching environment for those welfare children was better than neglect and street fighting. They would never know a perfect summer.

When my children stumbled off the plane after an eight-month absence from me, they were cranky crosspatches, weary of travel and adult emotion. My daughter was shy, my son did not recognize me. Their companions for that summer were four-year-old black children of similar dispositions. Emily helped in my classroom but by the end of the first week defected to an adjoining calmer room. My unrest seemed to pollute the air. One little boy sat at his table all morning, did not touch the colorful blocks set before him, and each time the wall clock moved forward a minute, he startled at the sound and said: "Theh it go agin," his eyes popping wide.

But you have more important things to do than worry about your career, if you have one. Getting money, cash for the road. You must realize early, months in advance, that money will be needed for food, shelter, transportation, and child care until you can find a job. Forget Welfare and Aid to Families with Dependent Children. You will not be able to tap public funds. Social workers ask questions and pursue answers: Where is your husband? Why is he not helping? Your birth certificate? The children's birth certificates? There are no fictional responses that will suffice. Not having a paper record tells them you are not real, you are probably guilty of something. If you do not have months in which to gather cash, *do not vanish*. Wait until the next opportunity.

If you have three or four months, stop paying all bills except rent and utilities. Make a bill file. As the envelopes turn pink, then red, and the file gets hot, chuck the whole mess into the garbage can and start over with a new file folder. You may have been the fastest bill payer in the United States and the habit of being financially re-sponsible may be tough to break. There's something wondrously moral about paying what you owe. You feel clean and virtuous, without sin. It may help to lecture yourself in the morning shower. Use pompous terms like Higher Cause, Best Interest, etc., and when you get desperate—Someday I'll Pay Them Back. Most of my un-paid bills were from lawyers, some of whom were still tidying up our three-year, two-state, transcontinental custody case. When they pressed for payment I tried to be pleasant and thank them for their services but thought to myself, "If I had paid you well, you'd have won the case." Compared to my husband's, my earning power was small, and every cent went to lawyers or for transportation from one state to another, or for personal maintenance—food and shelter. I could borrow small sums from relatives but could not borrow from institutions. I had no credit. I had been a wife and mother.

You don't have to cringe and whimper. You can work double time, sixteen hours a day. Typing, survey work, addressing enve-lopes, driving a newspaper-distribution van, a school bus, wait-ressing, tutoring, drudging in a nursing home. Save every cent. Borrow more from relatives, any amount. My parents, that last summer, were anxious about the $3,000 bond they had paid to guaranty the children's return. They were bitter, tired of paying, weary of child care, and weren't at all sure they even liked me. I was a granite boulder on their heads. I was a leak in their life savings. If you can wangle a loan from a credit union, do so. Be bold and if all goes as planned, you won't have to pay back.

Take time to re-examine your decision, your reasons for flight. Is HE truly a villain? Did he abuse, batter, frighten, turn the children against you? Did you exaggerate? Provoke? Have you skills, training, brains, courage sufficient to provide for your children? Do you harbor a hope that you'll find another supporter-husband, live-in lover in L.A., N.Y., or S.F.? If "I don't know" pops into your mouth as answer to any of these questions, abandon plans and stay where you are.

YOU WILL HAVE NOTICED that in the preparatory stage you've begun lying. There will be a lot more lying in your future. You may remember that I said NEVER LIE TO THE CHILDREN. There is, however, a before and an after. While you are still in the life you are leaving, the Before, you will be acting a role. You are probably encouraging the children to talk on the phone to their father, you are discussing with him and with the children their return to his custody. You may even be planning with your lawyer a future court date. The children will ask questions. "Why can't we live with you, Mommy?" Because the judge says you can't. "Will you visit us when we go back to Father?" The judge will not allow that, but I'll write letters to you. Your mother says: "You're not planning anything stupid, are you?" No. Your sister says: "It's a damn shame. You'll let me know if I can help?" Yes. Thanks. I'm fine. I'm adjusting. Someone offers you a job for two months hence when you hope you'll be long gone. You accept. You sign a contract and keep in touch. You are practicing the art of lying.

You are also watching for signs that you are being tailed or tapped. If you have an accomplice, don't meet him or her for lunch or dinner and certainly not in your residence, and don't talk on the phone or write notes. Potential accomplices seem to pop up like the first crocuses through the melting snow, and not because you have solicited help. You are a visible Need, a bleeding victim, not quite dead. They offer transcripts, a dead cousin's diploma, advice, the use of a neutral automobile to get you to any destination. You shake your head and walk away. Before you accept any of these aids you must make sure your helper is not acting out of pity. He or she must demonstrate quiet pleasure in confounding authorities, in getting away with sabotaging society's legal system, and an anticipatory delight in lying to the FBI. These qualifications are more enduring than personal affection or sympathy with the victim. Don't confide details of the Plan to ANYONE.

Nowadays, forty years on, there is something new you must weave into your thoughts. Organizations with names like Vanished Children's Alliance or Missing Children's Network are forming to retrieve children. No distinction is made, except in their files, between children who have been scattered by custody battles and those whose disappearance cannot be explained and whose mother and father keep a mute vigil over an empty bedroom. The public is an interested national posse that feels comforted by supermarket bags bearing tragic statistics, pictures on graffitied subway walls, airline terminal benches. I cannot make this less serious than it is. No citizen or child can hide from TV. Be cautious.

Do not enter your child at mid-term in a public school. Tell a good story, elongate your neck until your head touches the clouds, let the children's hair grow, avoid baby-sitters, and, with a smile, walk away from neighbors. Time will pass and the faces on the bags will change. There are so many missing children. Soon the public's pirouette into altruism will change into a more stately dance and will begin to concentrate on children whose disappearance cannot be explained by ". . . her father took her. . . ." Women will begin to notice that in the news stories about children who have been found as a result of a TV picture, an unseemly number of distraught mothers are dragged back to face the judge. They will learn that 70 percent of the fathers who ask for custody *get* it, and they will begin to ask why. In the meantime you can't constantly act as though you are hiding. It's not good for the children. You might as well walk proudly and make sure the child takes your hand when you cross a busy street.

YOU MUST DECIDE WHERE YOU ARE GOING. Will it be a warmer place or have you chosen North Dakota on the assumption that people are too busy with the weather up there to notice irregularity? My choice was Tucson, a mistake, and one I had sense enough to rectify after two weeks. 107 degrees. No public kindergartens. You cannot just take off and hope for the best. You may like the ocean and feel safe in nature, but wherever you go, you will be entering a community and you must seek, at the least, an indifferent population, at best, an economically prospering hive that will deliver you a means of support. A place, in short, that is paving the land with gas stations on four corners, where flower acreage is yielding to supermarkets, where condos get permits on prime land and the Chamber of Commerce building is two minutes from the freeway.

The best way to find out about a place is to ask those who have been there, but this method of research is not safe for one who wishes to vanish. You are playing the role of resigned victim and you can't strike up conversations about Spokane or Butte without arousing suspicion. What's left? Books? It is not safe to go carelessly to a library or bookstore. You must assume your actions are being observed. If this sounds like paranoia, sometimes the tiger is a real tiger and in court I've heard my most innocent remarks relayed, with innuendo, into the ears of an impatient judge.

If you use a library, don't check out a travel book. Find a private place for reading and when you've collected a few books, do your reading swiftly. Before you leave, put the travel books back on the shelves, out of order. If you browse at a bookstore, don't idle at the travel section. Remove the book that interests you and read it in the poetry corner. This skulking is good practice and should not depress you. You're training your mind and body to act with caution and you're learning to divorce your demeanor from the contents of your mind. You are becoming an actress, and high time! Remember the time so long ago when you naively believed the state could not take from you the children who had split your body and sucked milk from your breasts? Remember the office where you said this, your eyes wide and brimming with tears? What a ridiculous, pathetic, stupid, ignorant, whining, weak lump you were! Notice how poised, serene, and self-confident you appear now as you step down the library stairs, the knowledge in your head, no notes left behind or in your purse. You may even be sassy enough to check out two books on London and pause beside your car to read a few pages. If you can't as yet wholeheartedly love this new woman, try at least to admire her art.

With your destination to guide you, you are now ready to select those items you want to accompany you on your journey. You are not going to throw clothes into boxes at the last moment, struggle with them to the getaway car with children, bewildered, crying, asking questions. You are going to begin making choices weeks in advance, and your imperatives will be Need and Minimum. Need can stretch a bit to include items of beauty with no function (a hand-carved angel, a tiny Buddha, a throw of red wool with interwoven golden thread) or pictures of the children, parents, or objects of psychological importance to your hostages—a teddy bear, a blanket. You should, however, keep your mind on the place beyond and try to picture yourself going in and out, wearing those pants or that dress, walking in those shoes, the children inconspicuously dressed in J.C. Penney clothes. Forget your wedding china, your great-aunt's petit-pointed footstool, the brass sherry decanter that contains a music box in its base. "Skaters' Waltz."

I kept three paper cartons on the top shelf of my bedroom closet. They were labeled in black magic marker ink "Household," "Children," and "Self" and beneath each label I printed "O.P." No snoop could possibly guess that O.P. meant Operation Powder. Each time I climbed onto a chair to place a garment or object in one of the three boxes, my knees turned into cottage cheese, my hands trembled, my throat swelled, and I felt as though I were collecting the effects of people who had just died. This was always late at night in my court-allowed one summer month, when the children were asleep. One night the chair tipped me into a heap on the floor and the chair became omen, forecasting slippage and chance collapse of all Plan.

And I want you to know that there is a lie in what I write, in the larky tone and jaunty, bold recall. I was not the gay adventurer I wanted to be. I was ill with fear, demented, during all those days of preparation. I wasn't sure there was enough clay left to shape me into a new woman.

. . .

THE CHILDREN AND I LEFT TOWN in a borrowed car at the end of August 1965. I turned the radio dial to all stations as we covered the miles. Each station gave out news of the Watts Riot in L.A. There was no news of a vanishing woman.

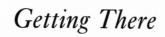

Getting There

The first day of school, September 8, 1971. Seven-fifteen a.m. Lunches packed for them. Goodbye and kisses to Emily and Louis. "Lock the gate. Put the cats out. Don't miss your bus. Love you!" A big hug from Louis, a look of "Here we go again" from Emily. (I must spend more time with her this year, be more tolerant of her junior-high miseries, talk more with her, avoid seeing myself in her.)

Time enough to run to the beach, two houses down the lane. There it is, infinite, generous with its gifts of changeless character, purpose on earth, beauty. Like the ice weed surrounding the house, each day my body takes in nourishment from sea spray and hot or cold sand on my bare feet. The ocean tells me something about endurance, change, cycles, and style, all of which I need, every day, in teaching and mothering. Each day I thank her for her help, not out loud, in the blood.

As I walk towards my red VW, old Squareback, I remember the smashed front. Dear Principal, I'm very sorry I couldn't make it to your Sunday open-house yesterday, in honor of the district's first year of integration and busing. You see, on the freeway a Dodge truck aimed itself at me, struck, and the rest of the afternoon was police, tow truck, insurance companies, nerves. I'm five minutes away from the salt spray on my face and already I'm thinking budgets, the rent increase in August, the district's salary freeze, Emily's teeth, Louis's passion for expensive karate. My breakfast egg with granola on top is now a stone in my stomach. "Fuck it," I say to myself. This expletive is a poisoned dart; it zips out and rips U.S. presidents, orthodontists, principals, insurance companies, landlords, a sweet stoned hippie in an incensed Dodge truck, bank clerks, bill collectors. Uttered at seven-thirty on a school day, it will, if luck holds, bulldoze for me a path for six or seven hours. Its effectiveness varies inversely with frequency of use. Value derives from scarcity and the social contract which legislates that lady schoolteachers never use such language.

Four-year-old Danny from next door is standing in front of the car, eyes wide. "You got smashed?" He drops his toy gun onto the street and fingers the splintered glass in the socket of the headlight. "Was you bloody?" Danny's mother is a waitress. She works until midnight and sleeps late every morning. Danny knows everyone four or five lanes north and south, and hours before the alarm wakes me each morning, Danny already knows there is a dead seal or jellyfish on the beach, that the street workers left the key in the Caterpillar ignition, that the swallow's nest fell off the wall, and that leftover chocolate cake with canned whipped cream tastes better than Rice Krispies for breakfast. Chocolate is smeared on him like black-face.

"Watch that glass, Danny."

"We have a new color TV. It cos' thousands. Millions!"

"Danny, when are you going to come to school again with me?"

"Now."

"No, you can't come in your pajamas. You get up early tomorrow morning, get dressed, and come knock on our door. Wear shoes. Ask your mother. 'Bye!"

It's seven-forty-five and I'm fifteen minutes late to pick up Sharon. Halfway down the lane I wave to Mr. Wooley, who is carefully wiping dew from his windshield, paper towel in one hand, attaché case in the other. He wipes a 5" by 8" rectangle, then another, same size. He teaches at the college, has a French wife, and isn't friendly. Mr. and Mrs. Wooley have flawless tans, expensive white bathing suits, and each afternoon they jog together down to the beach. I stare as they pass my living-room window.

At the end of the lane Mr. Retired-Petroleum-Engineer sweeps his driveway and leers at me. The new brick wall he has built around his retirement house to keep out the new generation is so high his wife can't see over it to watch him.

I turn left onto the boulevard. At the corner is the yellow bus loading children for Cabrillo Junior High School, uptown, across the freeway. The boys stand apart, some of them furtively/casually smoking, touching free space between home and school. The girls are in small clusters, binders hugged to their chests. Every style represented: blue jeans, maxis, minis, granny gowns, shorts, sandals, sneakers, square heels, bare legs, pantyhose. Emily stands aloof, apart. Sharp memory of myself, etched with separateness. Although the day is already warm, she wears a winter red plaid skirt, a black sweater, white knee-socks, white sneakers, her long, sheaves-of-wheat hair topped with a red angora tam. Little face, too thin, pale even after a summer in the sun. Her friend Debbie, sister of Danny, is standing near her, triumphant in a shimmering sleeveless blouse, new breasts pushing out her padded bra, long bare tanned legs in a mini-skirt of Taiwan plastic, square heels. Debbie is watching the boys. Emily is watching the middle distance and trying to be the last to board the bus, afraid of the physical crush at the back. She catches sight of me and wanly waves me on. I cannot receive the blows in her place. She has to get tough. I cannot buy popularity for her. (When I was about ten, I wanted to be the friend of a certain popular girl, to be chosen by her to receive her secrets. Her name was Dolores Kilingstad, a new arrival at our school from the wicked, sophisticated California Southland. She wore lipstick and her hair was artificially curled. She was pale, thin, and carried real money in a purse. She couldn't remember my name, called me "You there." We were a nutrition-minded family.

We never had candy right out there on a table for someone to eat. It was always hidden, usually at the top of my mother's closet, behind the hat boxes. If I swiped one piece a day, no more, she wouldn't notice. I took four chocolate creams and one chew. The candies in their brown fluted paper wrappers fit perfectly into a tiny golden box from a Tiddlywinks game. A silver string to tie around it. A sprig of lavender stuck under the string. It had taken me all week to steal the bribe and a weekend of hiding it under my panties in my bureau drawer. On Monday morning, heart pounding, I offered it to Dolores. In five minutes, she received the present, opened it, passed the chocolates around to her admirers, ate one herself, threw the lavender and the box and string into the ashcan, and turned her back. On Tuesday morning, she said to me, "You there, that's a pretty bracelet you have. May I see it?" I swam to her side, holding up my thin brown arm. "Take it off," she said. I took it off. She put it on her pale wrist. "May I have it?" I nodded. It was GOLD with silver charms and I loved it, never took it off, even in the bath. Again she walked away, laughing with her friends, not unkindly, not *at* me, but separate from me. Would Emily like to hear how craven I was?)

The VW idles in front of Sharon's box-house, while Sharon and her husband Jerry open the back and load three brown bags and one cage. They hug, which dislodges Sharon's broad-brimmed black velvet hat. She giggles, a high tee-hee-hee, unique to Sharon. As she tugs at the passenger door, I realize it no longer will open. I get out and let her in from the driver's side. "They really fucked you, didn't they?" she mutters as she squeezes her long skirt under the wheel, one suede cowboy boot over the gear shift, her plump bottom plop, into the seat, right hand on her hat, second cowboy boot follows, the khaki canvas Army canteen shoulder bag trailing behind on the driver's seat.

"Good morning, Sharon, funky new bag!"

"Got it at the swap-meet last week. We collected crud and crap out of the garbage cans and sold it all for $33 . . . oh, I love those swap-meets . . . you meet such nuts. And that's where the hat was, just there waiting, I couldn't not buy it. $1.50. Some old ballet dancer was selling her props . . ."

Wind her up and let her run, my accompaniment as I drive to work. James Agee says: "Most young writers and artists roll around in description like honeymooners on a bed." Sounds okay to me. I'll start at the top of her. She wears glasses and is blind without them. They are tinted a golden sherry color, round, with metal rims. When she takes off her glasses to clean them she seems to be removing her face. Her head is round, like the heads on the cherubs in the Campbell's Soup ads, and her light copper hair flows down her back almost to her waist; it is thin and straight, worn parted in the middle, kept out of her eyes by the two strands tucked behind her ears. Her white, white skin is lightly freckled and subject to rashes and eczema patches. Mouth and nose and ears delicately made, dainty, feminine. Her teeth are yellowish and fragile. No makeup.

From the neck down, she's a female out of "Bonanza," God Funk is her tailor. This morning she's fitted into a colonial-blue maxi-dress, with a white lace-patterned print. The waist is nipped in, the skirt gathered but tapered at the ankles. The sleeves are full over the upper arm with insets of ruffled Newberry lace, fitted to the wrist, edged in lace. The neckline is square and cut as low as she can get away with. I note she's wearing a bra, a self-imposed restraint for school only. On her feet are battered, dirty, ill-fitting, pointy-toed cowboy boots, which suggest she had to slog it through a foot of mud to get to the tavern or feed the chickens. Around her neck hangs a long piece of thong with an ugly stainless steel whistle attached. It bounces up and down over the breast precipice as she talks.

"Oh-oh, I'm not ready to *do* today, are you? The open-house yesterday was fucked. All those Anglo parents looking me over and asking about curriculum. 'My Eddie already knows the alphabet and I hope he won't be held back over here'—so I explain and explain about grouping and individualized instruction and how there will be three adults in the classroom at all times and they say: 'Three?' and I say: 'Yes. Myself. Marcia, the other Kg. teacher, and Raquel, the aide.' 'Oh, Raquel,' they say, looking right through her. Fuck them. I *hate* Anglos. And I hate their children!"

"Now, now," I soothe.

"And that Marcia. I just don't know where she is, can't figure her out. She's divorced and has two children and the guy she's going to marry is divorced and has two children and she won't sleep with him until they get married, in *November!* And she said she didn't mind pets in the classroom as long as they didn't stink or make a mess and I took her seriously and worried and worried and then found out she was *kidding* me. And she's all jittery and keeps showing me cute little ditto sheets and projects for the kids to do and won't let me cover the walls with yellow burlap, and she has all these dopey songs for the kids to learn . . ."

The nasal lament continues, background for my thoughts, like the noise of the VW engine coming through the floorboards, the whir of cars passing me on the harbor road. I don't have to pay attention to engine noise unless there's a new, unusual sound. Sharon's subterranean monologue is as natural to her as a mockingbird's constant comment; it comforts me.

We turn left off the ocean highway. From ocean to school is almost a straight line through irrigated farm land (65 miles an hour), past the city dump turnoff, through new tract housing developments (40 miles an hour), past a new shopping center (20 miles an hour) to the stoplight at State Highway 1, at the railroad tracks. Make what Sharon calls a "California right turn" through the red light, then a left turn with the green light across the tracks just behind the yellow school bus carrying Anglos for the first time into the barrio. I am curious and I stare at the children. Ten more blocks (10 miles an hour) through the familiar congested, ugly, crowded, humming, government-subsidized squalor of our adopted tenement, where Sharon and I can exist each day without being destroyed by our own frailties and prejudices. Past Guadalupe Church and School, turn right at stop sign (5 miles an hour), and we are There.

One more moment before we insert ourselves into the public school envelope.

"Where the fuck are my keys—did Jerry take them?—where—oh, do I *have* to *do* this day?" Sharon finds her keys at the bottom of her new purse. My keys are where they always are, pinned to my straw purse. I unpin them, pin them again to my slacks pocket. I put the car keys in the glove compartment and leave the car unlocked. A game of risk and trust.

Mom Wants to Write

It is a summer morning in Southern California and I am at the typewriter, coffee to the right, cigarettes to the left. At six a.m. my two children gaily and loudly drove off with a trusted driver to visit friends 500 miles north, because "Mom wants to write." They will be away from me for five days. I have promised myself that during their absence I shall not avoid the typewriter, but already I have stayed quite clear of it for five hours.

There are many things I could be doing which would be so much more fun. I could be washing the dishes or cleaning the house. I could be walking on the beach, viewing the plankton influx which last night brought phosphorescent green white-caps and sparked my footsteps in the sand. I could read one of the new Sturgeon paperbacks brought to me yesterday by a teacher-friend. I could bicycle to the store, select a new Clairol color slightly less garish than the present Golden Blonde, and mix it into my tortured hair. I could go out in the backyard and talk to the man who is digging up the brick patio and the lawn in a serious search for the cause of leach-field overflow. I could garden or just sit and stare at two lizards, three cats, five kittens, three hens, one bantam rooster, and two guinea pigs, justifying the sitting and staring by discovering whether their pecking order ever varies. I could look at all the dead snails and slugs, victims of Snarol. I could iron for an hour or two and re-discover clothes I haven't seen for a year, let down or take up a dress hem, though I never wear dresses.

Mom wants to write but perhaps I shall simply list my time-wasting activities in the next four days. A woman is defined by what she *does*, not by what she feels or thinks. Clairol buying is one of the things I do, like teaching and kissing children goodnight.

I FLED THE TYPEWRITER FOR TWO HOURS. I drove a battered 1982 VW to a fancy shopping plaza, where I bought a pair of size nine navy-blue slacks, a bit too small, and a bright blue cotton pullover a bit too large to cover the bit-too-small portion of the slacks. I also bought a yellow and orange madras bedspread for my double bed. While I wandered among the fashionably dressed shoppers, I compared myself to them and felt ugly. I was deliberately slouching around in a pair of brown tacky velour pants and a faded madras top of unidentifiable color. My hair was not quite combed and as usual I wore no lipstick or makeup. Whenever I caught sight of myself in one of the cruel mirrors I winced and turned away. "I refuse to compete," I told myself. Nevertheless, I had just bought two garments quite definitely in fashion.

HOME AGAIN AT THE TYPEWRITER, I remember my reason for sending my children away. Mom wants to write. Mom has written a few stories, unpublished. She has written four pedagogical articles, distributed but not published. Mom does not enjoy writing and all acts of writing are endured only because accompanied by a motif of self-delusion—"I write, therefore I am a writer. A writer is an artist. I am an artist. An artist is more than Woman, more than Teacher, more than Mother."

THIS EVENING I JOINED MY TUESDAY EVENING Balkan dance group, then down the hill on my bicycle, the wind cooling the perspiration on my body, to the beach community where I live. A dark lonely house. A telephone call from my children, already linked to new activities with different people, a potter's wheel nearby, a hayloft where they will sleep in sleeping bags, bats swooping in the dark. I take a cool bath where I once again observe detachedly the jagged scar running from ribcage to shoulder on the left side of me, where once there was a breast to match the right side of me. Rubdown with avocado-colored towel, tiger kitten biting my toes.

Bra with dime-store foam rubber insertion. Nylon tricot pajamas. Dislike being asymmetrical.

Nightly ritualistic tour of the backyard, stepping carefully this evening between the piled patio bricks and the septic-tank holes. Chanticleer, the rooster, asleep in the tree with one of his hens. He is not monogamous. I reach up high to lift him free of the twigs and carry him to the cage with tent flap over it to muffle his cries at five in the morning. His golden wings flap in the moonlight and his comb looks like a wound. Dampness and sea smells. A slug in the wet grass under my bare heel. Two pull-ups on the metal bar that supports the clothesline because a year ago my son told me my upper arms were getting flabby. I am young, strong and beautiful. Forty-six years old. Old.

I WAKE UP and can see everything clearly in the flickering light. Not electric light. The pleasant soft orange of a campfire. The luminous clock face says four. I go to the kitchen where the window is a frame for silent flames just beyond the cluster of trees where Chanticleer sometimes sleeps. I step outside. Heat. There is no sound except mother cat's meow as she slips by me to her babies in a box beside my son's bed. There is a faint tinkling of glass like my grandmother's crystal wind chimes, then a more distant cry of "Fire!" I climb on top of a pile of patio bricks and I estimate the fire's distance at no more than fifty feet. Fire and I are separated by trees, a playhouse, an old wooden fence, a chicken cage, and grass. From far away my mother's voice says to me: "Don't ever go to a fire!" Fire has come to me and it's the greatest show on earth. Now I hear the faint wail of the fire siren and am triggered into practicality. What shall I do? Let Chanticleer out of his cage. He and his hens can fly away. Make sure mother cat is out of the house, never mind the newborn kittens. She can make more. Open the gates for the guinea pigs.

Possessions? Clothes? But I never can decide what to wear on an indifferent day. How am I to choose now when I may have to live in the garments for a week? Funky velour pants and faded madras top. Beige wool poncho knit by a friend. Get two-teeth bridge from bathrobe pocket and put it in my mouth. Bra, put it on. Papers from the typewriter. Baroque wooden angel over my bed. Purse with cash. Already I have chosen.

As I watch Fire, I list to myself some of the items I shall leave behind to burn, parts of me I've mixed my labor with. Ten file drawers of teaching materials in the closet, so ill-organized that years of teaching pass and I do not sort and use. Hundreds of original typed exercises for use in the classroom. Educational reference books. The Steinway upright that I use to tune the guitar. The guitar and all the music. The stereo, the records, the Robeson 78s. Clothes, dishes, bureaus, beds, tables, chairs. A catalogue of me, a collection of dreams and intentions and failures and partial pleasures. I am tempted to scoop up the children's art work—the rooster etched in copper, the girl's self-portrait, the boy's Rube Goldberg drawings—but there is so much of it and all is precious. The girl will never forgive me for abandoning the newborns and I hastily include them in my take-and-flee list, fearing her brimming, accusing eyes.

Fire engines, hoses through my backyard, twenty-five or thirty neighbors all telling favorite fire horror tales. Six police cars, one ambulance with stretcher placed on my doorstep, flashing red lights, radio communication . . . "Is anyone in that house?"

We're all pleased to be outside in our pajamas in a warm summer dawn witnessing an outbreak of nature and another's misfortune. But alas, no one is in that house and the firemen work swiftly, dousing flames with gallons of water. Fire is dead. Again it is dark. We linger a while in a nocturnal community of feeling, then politely retreat from one another, closing our doors.

I go back outside and perch for an hour on a pile of patio bricks and watch the men finish the task. I am not curious about the hoses or the engine or the extinguishing agents, but I search the secret of the hive mind that seems to be linking these twenty big males. They all look exactly alike—tall, lean, fit, and Anglo. There is no doubt, indecision, wonder, or fear. They don't talk or trip over each other or duplicate effort. There is no "shit" or "fuck" or even "damn" as one after the other trips over a brick or stumbles into a hole. They might be androids.

THE NEXT DAY, in the afternoon Danny from next door somehow gets into the house and invites me to go swimming. "Danny! Can't you see I'm WRITING? I can't go swimming now!"

"Why not?" he asks. "Don'cha have a bathin' suit?"

"No."

"Don'cha have some shorts?"

I look him over carefully. After all, it is hot and he's only four and won't notice, or care much if he does notice, wrinkles, blotches, varicosities, a gouged shoulder, a lack of symmetry. I put on shorts underneath my velour pants, with a sleeveless top, grab a towel, and run with Danny over the hot sand to the water's edge, double back to dry sand, spread out my towel, take off my pants and sit down. Danny races himself into the water, then runs back to me.

"Do you know how to skin?" he asks "Ya wanna learn? I'll teach you. Watch me." Little legs sprint towards the water and at the last moment the heels dig in and he's in for a homerun.

"That's not a skin, it's a *skid*," I say.

"Yeah, skin. Wanna try it?"

"Yes! I wanna try it!" I stand up, aware of defects, beckoned by Danny's expectant smile, lured by the water sparkling on his brown skin, and I run to the water, fleeing from, racing towards. I try to skin, but sit down hard with water and sand cupping my buttocks like a man's strong hands. Danny, water, sun. Leap, jump, run. Jump-rope with seaweed strand. Chase that boy, let him chase me. Run to the jetty. Climb up barnacled man-made stone, scrunch down into a cave, poke anemones, watch them suck a stick, chase crabs, squeal when water closes in, leap out onto sand. Run to dry warm sand. Lie on stomachs. Cover over all parts of us with hot granules. Up again and into the water. Lie on backs and watch clouds.

"Do you know how to swim, Danny?"

"Yeah, but I'm not gonna show you."

DANNY, YOU'RE A LIAR. You don't want me to know you can't swim. I understand because I don't want anyone to know how much I think about aging and decay. You could learn to swim, you shall learn to swim. Perhaps I could even teach you. And surely I can learn to talk about wrinkles and take off the cheery mask I wear, remove it once in a while, like my two-teeth bridge and my foam rubber.

Danny wanders away from me following a stray dog. I don't have to watch him, but I do. I know his waitress mother is asleep and has no idea where he is, but experience (he's still alive, isn't he?) has shown her that Danny can take good care of himself. Here

comes Mr. Wooley in white trunks jogging down the beach. He has
that self-righteous look of all dedicated joggers, that blind I-am-
one-with-God stare. Maybe, surely, he'll go right by me, but just
to be sure, I'll turn on my stomach and fake sleep. The sand trans-
mits the thump of his footsteps and they're slowing down.

"Good afternoon! [hearty! wouldn't you know it?] May I sit
down?"

(No—this is my afternoon—don't climb in!) "Sure. Why not?
Getting your afternoon exercise?" (Human speech, for the most
part, is calculatedly asinine. Next he's going to say: "It's a nice afternoon. We don't often have sun this time of year.")

"It's a nice afternoon. We don't often have sun this time of
year," he says. His only deviation from a TV commercial is his
mouth. His bite is wrong; the upper teeth hang over the lower jaw
giving him a weak gopherish face. While I'm looking at him, he's
looking at me. I hope all the defects terrify him and he goes screaming in fear of imminent decay and death, stumbling over the sand,
to fall gasping into the arms of his perfect French wife. He settles
into the sand. I'm suddenly feeling very tired.

"I saw you playing with Danny. It looked like fun. That kid
needs someone like you to take an interest in him. He just runs
loose all over the neighborhood. He's only four, isn't he?"

"I dunno. He's giving himself an education. Do you teach at
the college?"

I already know he teaches at the college, but I want to change the subject. I don't want to beat up on Danny or his mother when they're not around.

"I teach industrial arts and P.E. There's no father in the home, is there? I've seen him *six* blocks away from home looking for bottles in garbage cans. He *plays* on the tractors after the workmen go home. He could get hurt. And when they're working he's always out there watching. He might get run over. Lots of times I've just missed hitting him myself." He looks more and more like a gopher, gnawing at the roots of a plant.

"I don't think it's as serious as you're making it seem. He has several sisters who usually know where he is when his mother is working. Don't worry about it." I try to seem neutral.

"I doubt if they know where he is. I just want to say that I've worked with fatherless boys who have been neglected by their working mothers. I know it's hard on them—hard on the mothers too—and the courts are full of these kids who grow up without any guidance, and then just run wild . . ." He's warming up to his subject and I'm wanting to squash him. *My* children are fatherless and *I'm* a working mother. How am I going to shut him up?

". . . and I think the authorities should know about it."

"Wait a minute, slow down. Hilda works as a waitress, long hours at night, to support five children. Her girls know how to cook and take care of the household. They gather Danny in and feed him, wash him, put him to bed. Hilda may not know where he is, but *I* know he's walking down the beach with a dog, and most of the people on our lane know what he's up to most of the day. He doesn't steal things or break windows. He knows little old ladies for blocks around. Are they complaining? The worst thing I ever saw him do was run up and down the lane one day spraying Raid at everything in sight. But most of the people I know do that and call it control or hygiene. I think we should mind our own business."

I pull on my velour pants. I'm trembling and hope it doesn't show. What this country needs is a wipe-out. I should never have left the house. My romp with Danny, all water-sparkled and sunny and warm, is now overcast with gray clouds, and for the first time since I've known Danny, I fear for his safety. It's earthquake weather, as my mother used to say, and I miss my children.

BACK AT THE TYPEWRITER. Step-hop-turn and begin again. My young friend Michael, twenty-seven years old, wanders in through the screen door. I invite him to read the part about Danny. He says, sitting at the piano: "Here you are. Ape at a typewriter. It's not good enough. Elevate it! Tell the Danny thing in a poem and then make a song out of it and then put it back into words. All you're doing is diary, therapy. There's *got* to be more!"

I don't know anything for sure. I don't even know if small moths are generating themselves out of the unshelled peanuts resting in a wooden bowl on the kitchen table. I just saw a white worm crawling around the bowl's edge and I count four moths on the mound of peanuts. The whole mixture will have to go into the garbage.

Theodore Sturgeon said: "I write what I write to find a way home. I write long stories and short ones and angry ones and funny ones, so that they can be homes for me."

Mitterrand's Last Supper

Though I know what "tiny" means to the Beings, I don't know why they call me a "tiny songbird." I fit into a hand and then someone says: "Oh how tiny it is!" but no one seems to notice that from beak to the end of my body I measure about six and one-half inches. The sparrow is the same size and they don't call a sparrow tiny. When a Being says "tiny," oohs and aahs follow, and smiles of white teeth, and a Being who smells like a rose will say: "Oh let me hold it, please, please . . ."

I have a name given to me by the Beings. They name everything. My usual name is Ortolan Bunting but there's also a scientific name: *Emberiza hortulana*. No one calls me that and that's too bad for the Italian words fly and sing. Only once did I hear it spoken by a Being in a white jacket who was talking, talking in a room filled with Beings. I was there in that room about a moon ago and I was in a cage with other birds about my size. The Beings listening were learning how to make sure what they caught in their nets were Ortolans and not some other bird. That I was there being inspected meant I was near my end and even though I was not singing, I wasn't unhappy. I was healthy, fat, and eager to experience the final act of my life that I seemed to have learned from my mother. I have always known my fate and have spent my moons and suns doing what I had to do first, that is, breed.

You see, Ortolans are an "endangered species." I've heard this from many voices. It seems to mean that even though we migrate in flocks to places called Sardinia, or northern Africa, and there are so many of us, and we sing our seven notes ending in a "flourish," our numbers are getting fewer. When we fly these long distances of course we have prepared by getting fat and it's when we're fat that the Beings catch us in nets.

I've heard it said that we breed in Sardinia but that is not true. We find our mates in a place with a soft name, Lapland, where we are left alone and can grow fat by eating insects and seeds. We put our nests on the ground and soon there are six or seven, sometimes only five, eggs. Our eggs, glossy greenish white with purple and brown spots, are our future. We wait for the hatching and eat. We hope for at least five healthy young Ortolans so that each one of us will be able to fly south in autumn to take part in the Beings' ceremonies. We must be strong because we have two aims. Some of us must escape the nets and go to sing our songs in the warm gardens of Italy and France and then return north to breed again.

Others must submit gladly to capture and learn the meaning of their lives.

The nets are holes in the sky surrounded by thick string. When a net descends on us, we try to escape but there are so many of us, and we are crowded so close together, that our wings cannot spread and our voices can only slur and squeak. The wind cannot lift our bodies free. Sometimes our legs get broken, even torn from our bodies, and our tail feathers tangle and fall to the bottom of the net. We are frightened but we know we are on the journey, and we've been chosen. We are the Chosen Ortolans, the Chosen Birds, and we no longer have to strive to mate, to breed. It's true that we no longer sing, but singing happens in gardens or in the wide air, and we know that once we are in a net, we will live in rooms, in cages, waiting.

I don't believe I'll have to wait much longer. I'm in a cage with eleven other birds who are as fat as I am. The cage is in a dimly lighted room with a long table spread with a red tablecloth. There are twelve chairs, six on each side. Beings are entering the room one by one. They don't talk, they seem to shuffle, and since it is warm, they are dressed in light colors, in fabrics which seem scarcely to touch their skin. The skin on their faces bubbles in the heat. The Hosts are seating the visitors and opening for each a large black cloth and laying it on the red table covering.

I should tell you what has been happening to me since my capture in a net. I can't name the place for I didn't hear it spoken. Ortolans fly long distances but we don't name the destinations. I know only that the air was warm and that huge noisy birds flew down to the ground and Beings emerged from openings in the sides of the birds and gathered the nets filled with us, dragging them along the ground, which caused some of us to die and miss our most precious end. When that happened there was shouting and angry words spoken. "Jesus! Fuck it! Watch what the fuck yer doing!" and "Bon dieu de merde!" and "Stronzolos!" I was carried in the net to the huge bird and then I heard the openings clang shut and a terrible roar for a long time and then silence. It was dark and I couldn't move much because other Ortolans pressed their warm bodies against mine; we all tried again and again to lift our wings until we grew so tired I believe we slept.

Next, there was a thump and my net was carried out the openings, down the stairs to the ground. I looked closely at the Beings' bird but I saw no feathers and the wings were still spread from its body. My net was carried into a building and we were set free, free to enter a dark cage. I heard someone say we would be in the cage "twelve or more days" and I believe that means twelve suns. There is seed, "millet" they call it, all around us on the floor of the cage and since we've nothing else to do, we eat and eat. We know we must get as fat as possible. Beings visit and talk about the approaching "experience." They say again and again that the Ortolan is a "table delicacy" and they gather their fingers to their lips and smile. Beings who smell like jasmine sometimes pick me up in hands with red polished ends and stroke my feathers. They look into my eyes and one even kisses my beak. They comment on my colors which are fading. One says, "Gray head, lovely soft yellow throat, a good combination for a spring wardrobe."

Now, in the room with the long table, the twelve chairs, the red cloth, and the black napkins, I know I have only a short time in which to describe our moments of communion with Beings. I'm lucky, though sad to have to wait my turn, because six Ortolans are being taken from the cage and I can see what happens to them. Each bird stands on a table and a Being with an eyedropper lets one drop of Armagnac enter the open beak and then the bird falls over dead. Swiftly, but very carefully, six Beings pull every feather from the birds with implements called tweezers. This requires skill because no part that is inside can be allowed to ooze out. When all the feathers are removed and cast into a large container, the birds are placed inside an oven and roasted for five minutes. It is then that I smell the indescribable fragrance of roasted Ortolan. It is composed of the odor of air, the sea, the grasses where we built our nests, the newly hatched. Millet, as background.

Then everything happens almost too fast to see and understand, though I've known from my hatching time that this exquisite end is to be mine. Unless I have been eaten by a hawk, or have flown away from my flock, they will swallow my body, chew my bones, and drink my blood. Six Beings seat themselves at the long table. A Host Being instructs them to place the black napkins on their heads, letting them droop down over their faces. The Host Being says: "The napkin traps the fragrances, you will salivate and you must hold the Ortolan by its head and take the whole body into your mouth. It will be very hot! Are you ready?"

The heads nod yes, and into each hand a baked Ortolan is placed. I cannot see inside the napkin tent but the Host Being keeps on talking, almost whispering. He walks up and down behind the seated eaters. "Don't forget to cool your mouth with wine while you eat. And notice that in one part there are rich fatty flavors! In another part there is breast meat and bone. Different textures. The breast is succulent, refined. The tail is sensual, cerebral! The entrails . . . a combination of delights! Don't hurry. Savor every second. You are meeting your Chosen Ortolan and you will henceforth seek communion again and again. You will seek it across the oceans in America, you will deny that it happened, but you will know that it did happen and that you are changed. Bon appetit! Blessings on you."

Now it is my turn and my heart is beating fast. I smell the wine, the fat from our cooked bodies, the insistent odor of the warm Beings. The eyedropper is lifted and I eagerly open my beak.

See "Tiny Songbird Lands on the Plate at a Secret Chefs' Dinner in France," by Marian Burros, *New York Times*, Living Arts section, December 31, 1997.
Also see "Hold the Bird by Its Head," by Jon Carroll, *San Francisco Chronicle*, date not known.

Sartorial Notes on a Man I Knew

Once upon a Time,

May He Rest in Peace

In 1949, he wore World War II Officer pants, tailored to sleek fit, no pleats, of a material close to gabardine, but heavier, of light brown. Above the pants, in cool weather, a turtleneck of soft cotton, usually navy blue, tucked into the pants.

In warm weather, white Oxford button-down-collar shirts, tucked in, long sleeves turned up at the cuff, and over the shirt for classroom duty, a weathered Harris tweed sport jacket. All of his Oxford shirts were tailored to fit, with two tucks radiating from shoulder to below the waist. Socks, knit by his ex-wife, had to be washed by hand in gentle soap. The pants could not be washed. He was constantly taking them to the dry-cleaners or picking them up. The shirts had to be ironed perfectly and hung in the closet. He wore white boxer shorts and those had to be ironed as well.

He owned only one warm coat. This coat, he said, had been given to him by Henry Miller during a hopeful year-long residence in Big Sur when he was trying to write a novel. The coat was medium gray wool, decorated with moth feeding tracks, and so huge two people could fit inside it. The collar was large, folding back over the shoulders. From the generous yoke in back flowed yards of material down to his ankles. From center back, the gray belt of same material went forth in opposite directions, arrived in front, and after the coat was wrapped around him, could be casually tied. Except for the material, the coat looked like a bathrobe. We both were unrestrained in our admiration of this garment. It smelled of mothballs and tobacco.

He had, for rainy weather, a beige Burberry with no belt. He liked to carry with him a black umbrella which he often left wherever he'd just been and had to go back to claim. He used it like a cane and opened it only to protect his briefcase or books.

This was in California.

In 1950, on a humid, 100-degree afternoon, he attended the first gathering of new Princeton Ph.D. candidates, held outdoors in a garden. Drinks were served, wives were there in pastel sundresses; there were sandwiches cut in the shape of the Princeton triangle, visited by mosquitoes and flies. Everyone glistened with sweat. He wore, with his Officer pants and Oxford shirt, a vivid red-maroon light wool jacket, with gold buttons down the front (three on each side) and two gold buttons on each cuff. All the other men were either without jackets or wearing seersucker, gray and white. From the comments made, he learned that no one had worn red or maroon at Princeton in living memory. Everyone congratulated him on his bravado, his specificity, and mentioned his jacket first, then talked academic shop and ate and drank.

For Christmas, that first Princeton winter, his mother on the west coast sent him a suit she had had made from a length of material she had herself lovingly constructed on a loom. Construct is the right word because the material was stiff, thick, and refused to accept a crease. Jacket, pants (Officer style), and vest. The interwoven colors were navy blue, maroon, and beige. He wore it in cold weather but complained that the wool itched his legs and his crotch (his "balls") and it was much too warm as soon as he entered a building. He soon took to leaving the vest and pants carefully hanging on a special hanger in the closet and wearing the jacket occasionally, although he complained that the itch went right through his shirt to his shoulders and neck.

The second Princeton summer, he invested in a seersucker jacket, several pair of beige chambray cotton pants, and four expensive white Chinese cotton short-sleeved shirts. At home, he solved the heat problem by taking all garments off, or never putting anything on from early morning until he had to leave the house. His California sandals had rotted away the previous summer and he bought mesh sandals to wear outside. Inside our house, he went barefoot, and claimed that his toes were fungused. He would have liked to wear Bermuda shorts on campus (he had several pair) but no one wore shorts to class or to the library, except students, who sometimes took off their shirts and poured water or beer onto their hairy chests.

The third Princeton summer he lived naked in an overstuffed chair which oozed his sweat. He read all summer day and night and passed his exams in cotton pants and shirt, in brown hard leather shoes—for the occasion.

In early fall, having garnered funds from selling all of our possessions, except clothes, he bought a charcoal gray wool suit (no vest), the uniform, he had been told, of American scholars in Munich, where he was headed on a Fulbright grant. Also two white drip-dry nylon shirts which turned more gray with each washing.

In 1953, in Munich, he wore 4711 cologne, the favorite of Germans, and Arrid deodorant, used only by Americans, available at convenient PX stores.

In an elevator, in our newly built apartment, he faced another American who was wearing an identical charcoal gray suit, and each man was clutching a copy of David Riesman's *Individualism Reconsidered*.

During two Munich winters, he could be seen in his Henry Miller bathrobe-coat, on his bicycle, the excess cloth billowing out to the rear, a ski-mask of navy blue hugging his neck and ears. His mother's wool suit was again worn and no longer itched, perhaps because it was cold outdoors, and inside the underground library bunkers.

On a visit to Paris, he acquired a brown beret which he wore at sidewalk cafés and was often mistaken for a Frenchman, which pleased him.

When we traveled by train to Athens and Rome, we packed and wore only black outer garments that we purchased or borrowed on the theory that black wouldn't show dirt and we were traveling cheap. Our clothes got so dirty that simply wearing them turned our skin gray, dotted the pores black.

Back in the United Sates, with wife and two children and minimal academic wage, he wore the above garments, or in hot weather, nothing if indoors at home.

He did not, ever, wear jeans.

Sometime between 1956 and 1962 he added tennis clothes: white, white everything, shorts, T-shirts, Keds, socks. He retired his bathrobe coat which was a teepee shape and bought a heavy dark gray rectangle coat with enormous padded shoulders.

In divorce court in 1963, he wore smooth brown gabardine, Italian polished pointy-toe loafers, a white shirt with French cuffs, and a Countess Mara tie the color of cherry juice streaked with cobalt-blue lightning.

Comforter

I don't like the obituary form—all that attention given to the work
harness and family remainders, a shadowy begat list. I'd like to see a
new literary form appearing in the pages of the NY Times*—a rough,*
short, personal piece, written in grief, or relief—something remembered
from that life, a conversation, a friendship, a romance, or even a fight.
It should leak across two or four columns and be signed. It would not
have the shape of a tombstone or a coffin.

I was thinking about this when I wrote "Comforter."

T he women begin to spread the news.

Jay Leitschuh died last
night. He was flying his
Pterodactyl.

When?

Yesterday. About five.

YESTERDAY, about five, a
TORNADO touched down in Santa
Cruz, there was an inch of hail
around my house, the wind tried to
blow me off the hill, WHATINHELL
was he doing up in that machine?

I am angry and Kitty says yes it was foolish but we cannot
know all things. Kitty specializes in channels to the unknown but

now she's being practical and wonders if I can make it to a school memorial. I tell her I have a dental appointment in forty-five minutes but promise to visit what's left of Barbara before the sun goes down.

All day I think of flying machines, of Jay, of Barbara. I tell everyone I meet (the dentist, the grocery clerk) that Jay is dead and that he taught stained-glass to children and was just crazy about flying. They ask what was he doing up there in the air with a fragile craft when Nature so obviously wanted to smash him, and my anger rises again and again. How can I visit Barbara while I'm so angry that Jay risked his gentle life?

I'm a dictionary person, not a good comforter. I've looked up words all my life, and at lunchtime I get busy with a dictionary. "Barbara" from barbarian, or "a mnemonic term designating the first mood of the first syllogistic figure, in which both premises and the conclusion are universal affirmatives." She'll need all the universal affirmatives she can get and I'll tell her the meaning of her name. Perhaps. I don't have to look up "Leitschuh." I know it means leading-shoe, but I prefer "lightshoe," which seems to suit a tall slim soft-spoken dark-eyed man whose hands wove glass into patterns which backed up against light, and whose feet soundlessly crossed rooms.

The day frees me at four in the afternoon. I walk slowly through the rain, up the paths, my Birkenstocks seeping muddy water over the edges. I call her name, "Barbara . . . Barbara . . ." Not loudly, afraid to disturb whatever reconstruction may be taking place. The school children have gone home but there are usually resident children who greet me from inside trailers, rickety cabins, domes, or from their dam-building in the creek. Today, they are all in their hiding places and no one rushes to tell me news. I open the door to the art-room and call again. In the larger schoolroom, with its high rough rafters, once more I call out. My voice is no louder than a hoarse whisper, but it travels dutifully back to me, having bounced over cabinets, sewing machine, against patched stained-glass windows, up to the loft and down over what Barbara calls "the reality-orientation" board—the month (March), the day's number (19), the day of the week (Friday), the number of children present (13). Not my reality, I said. Nor mine either, she said, but sometimes it helps.

I leave the school and walk across the bridge, away from the hill where I know Barbara has a plastic dome, towards Bill's shack. He's at his wheel, his clay hands guiding a bowl, his clay knees taut.

"Where's Barbara?" I ask.

"She was in the kitchen a while ago. She's around somewhere."

We look at each other but don't discuss. Last names are seldom used at this school but I remember that his is Boesevetter, which means bad weather. He's a potter, a tree surgeon, carpenter, handyman, car repairman. A few days ago he told me that he flew helicopters in Vietnam for three years.

"Picking up bodies?" I asked.

"No, transporting money from one place to another."

"Money? What for?"

"Money is always needed, even when people are dying."

"Oh. Did you like flying?"

"No," he said.

I turn away from him and retrace my steps, back across the blue bridge, then on up past the open-air kitchen which Jay and Barbara have tidied and categorized and beautified until one almost forgets that wind whips through and there's no hot water. Past the bathrooms which Jay and Barbara have kept clean, even installing a bulletin board on the theory that sometime during each day everyone will visit and read.

Their bridge across the foaming creek is a board lying in ropes attached to oak tree branches. I hurry with the danger. I slide in the mud when I step onto the riverbank. My blue socks are now as brown as my Birkenstocks. I call her name again just below the first dome. I call out the names of her twin daughters. Jessica! Jasmina! There's no answer and I head on up the hill towards the Aptos Shelter Systems contraption of canvas and PVC pipes contorted into triangles and hexagons, which is their bedroom. The flap is open but before I see Barbara, I smell incense and the rain mixes, perfuming my face, dissolving, sucking, pulling, weakening.

"Barbara! Are you there?"

"Yes, yes, yes, come in, is it you? Yes, come in!"

She is standing tall in the center of her dome, unfolding a sheet for their waterbed. The dome suddenly reminds me of cervical caps, blocking sperm. I have time to notice that although Barbara's face is scarred, her nose too large and stubby, her teeth gapped, her hair the color of dried mud, eyes a discouraging light-blue, all adding up to homely, today she is magnified and beautiful. She is crying, smiling, laughing in short bursts, jigging in place as she seals me in her arms, burying her face in my wet green sweater.

                     "Oh Barbara, I'm so, so sorry"

"He is here now with me / I feel him here"

                     "Such a dear man, sweet man"

"Good, good man, my poor poor baby"

                     "Whimsical . . . melodious voice"

"What am I to do / how can I live without him?"

                     "We'll all help you, all of us"

"He told me / here / a minute ago / it is all right / he is fine"

    She pulls away from me and plunges across the waterbed to tuck in the sheet on the opposite side. Her jeaned bottom, her slim hips. I move to the end of the bed to help her. Women making beds. Their bed. The frame he made and she rubbed with steel-wool and linseed oil. She snatches up the pale-blue comforter and hugs it to her breasts.

"He left me his comforter / Oh nothing will keep me warm. It's cold now in Santa Cruz. After the rain, the mud, losing the dog in the flood, the good weather is coming. Tomorrow it will be here. Why couldn't he wait? The worst was over / is over / was over / why couldn't he wait?"

"He loved flying."

"He loved flying more than he loved me / no he didn't love anything but flying / just flying / like Lindbergh / but Lindbergh had a real plane, not a dinky hang-glider with a motor on it and unicorn rudders / see the rudders / beautiful aren't they?"

She has placed two translucent red and blue rudders with pictures of unicorns at head and foot of the waterbed and I don't understand at first that these are the rudders off his plunging craft.

"Look at them / not a mark on them / and Jay smashed / he tried to pull out and go up, but the Pterodactyl wanted to bury its beak in the earth and the motor drove his spine into his head [her fist smacks her open palm] and broke his face / his arms / his legs / he was so strong / he lived a few hours / he tried to come back to me / no not to me / tried to come back. Oh, the place where he crashed / it was so beautiful / the yellow flowers / sourgrass which I chewed on to settle my stomach / up near where you live / he was going to take me there today / or the first day of sun."

I sit down on the end of the waterbed, my knees weak. I say what I'm thinking.

"Barbara, why the pterodactyl, a flying reptile?"

"A reptile? No, an extinct bird. Jay, in the space age designing stained glass, was an extinct bird." She pauses, suddenly calm. She sits down beside me.

"I've been going through his things, funny things, letters from women, flight logs. Lots of women loved him and I lost him many times, but now, now he belongs forever to me, is mine forever." She hugs his comforter.

I don't reply and know that she, being Barbara, will discard this thought, will in fact, perhaps tomorrow, begin to offer her Jay to others: here's an odd piece / listen to this / that's what he said / who he really was / didn't you know? / don't forget him. She stands up again, swaying her breasts in a rocking movement, clutching the white silk scarf with monogrammed "J" around her neck.

"I want a wake! Everybody come and sit out in the sun and tell loud how they loved him / so loud he can hear us / and his parents want him cremated / want me to send them some ashes / and then maybe one of the pilots will scatter the rest out at sea. We had four months / four perfect months / spooning in our bed / turning when he turned / I turned / one soul."

Jasmina bursts into the dome. She's in her usual state of disrepair, her yellow hair tangled, jeans dirty and wet, face streaked with mud, her bare arms covered by pink lotion and the scars from the poison-oak she has had all winter.

"Mom, I'm hungry. Let's go out to dinner."

"Sit down, honey, I want to talk to you."

Jasmina sees the rudders. "Oh, the rudders. They didn't work. We saw him trying to turn them."

"You saw him try? / not work? / why wouldn't they work? / that could be important!" Barbara balances her knees on the sloshing bed and pulls up the rudders, laying them flat on top of the sheet. She yanks on the cables. Jasmina picks up a battered yellow helmet.

"We had to cut the strap to get it off his head."

Barbara takes the helmet from Jasmina and peers inside. Her fingers stroke the edges.

"Jasmina—you were there?" I ask in a whisper.

"Yeah—so was Jessica, and Dan and a couple of fliers. Mom, I'm hungry, let's go out to dinner." Jasmina's eyes are looking at helmet, unicorns, my feet, the top of the dome, everywhere but at Barbara. Barbara grabs her hands.

"Jasmina, look at me. I'm feeling better now and I'm sorry I was so crazy last night. We don't have any money to go out to dinner. How about some spaghetti? Look / look / see what I have?" She picks up a plastic box from the shelf and shows us her treasure. "See, my baby's hair, wet from the rain / just a piece of it / curly / I'm going to save it."

Jasmina wrinkles her nose and backs away. "Save it? Why?"

"And tomorrow is his birthday and I didn't get him a present / knew he wouldn't be needing it I guess / but I have a cake and we'll celebrate and eat his cake."

"Celebrate? What for? Mom, I want to go back to Milwaukee. First the dog, and now my . . . Jay . . . and the rain and poison oak . . ."

"I don't know. Back to locks / crowded city / snow / but I'm afraid without Jay / was our protection / maybe / I don't know."

"How about if I take you out to dinner tomorrow night? Anywhere you like." At least I can feed them.

"Yeah. Eric's Deli. Milwaukee Special Sandwich," Jasmina says. Barbara stares at the rain through the open dome flaps.

"That'll be nice, real nice. Kitty said she talked to him this morning and he said he's all right and that he loves me and to take care of me."

"We'll all try. You have many friends here."

There's nothing more to say. I postpone talk until dinner tomorrow, and what shall I say then? I go back over the swaying plank across the creek and open the back door of the art room. There is a bird huddled in front of the desk. He startles when I enter and flies up to the window where Jay's stained glass is propped, out of harm's way. The bird tries to fly through the closed window, his wings knocking the glass into the sink below. I'll tell Kitty about the trapped bird and the broken stained glass. She'll know how to translate for tomorrow's memorial.

We're All in
This Together: A Memoir

The Day I Saw My Parents Naked

My parents' slow decline cannot be detected by the eye. On dutiful visits in the past, when I push the front doorbell—a special design for hard-of-hearing residents which sounds like amplified crickets—there is always Harry's voice and the tap of his rubber-tipped cane on hardwood floors. "ALL RIGHT! I'LL GET IT! OF COURSE IT RANG! CAN'T YOU HEAR THE DAMN THING?" After double locks click, he pushes the screen door in my face and I squeeze through. He is a trifle smaller in size but perhaps I'm imagining this, and he first wants to know why I'm late and Molly was worried and dinner is ready and do I want sherry before dinner, but there's not really enough time because it's six already and don't I know they eat at six?

Perhaps I've not visited for three months and although there have been alarming telephone calls and letters from Molly detailing small differences, everything looks and feels the same. The house smells of furniture polish and all the indoor plants seem to be doing fine. Molly walks—no, not a walk—she pushes her feet towards me. Is she looking more tired, more bent? Drier? I can't decide. I'm afraid to hug a being so fragile, and kissing her dry cheek is like pressing the last leaf of autumn to my lips. But her smile pushes all the wrinkles back to her ears and her hand on my arm is warm.

"My dear . . . so glad to see you . . . and you look so good. How *do* you do it? Still jumping?"

I must shout into the space between us. I try to bring them up to date on my life. I like to hide myself behind a story told indirectly, lazy talk, resisting Harry's insistence that a story have a point, preferably moral, or at least be newsworthy. I prefer ambiguity and density, like wild blackberry pushing through thistleweeds. With Harry beside me summarizing, and Molly facing me, her body tense as though she is commanding her chest or hands to become ears, my story splinters, pieces falling around me. Harry scoops up a piece. "Yes, even kindergarteners have real lives they want to talk about and the damn teachers won't let them." Molly says: "It must be hard, always to be fighting a system, but the children are fortunate in having you there." Was that what I was saying? I was trying to give bits of children's thought, the quirks of mind, the perversity of language, tiny chunks of nonsense to make my parents laugh. I fail. Molly's ears hear disasters and gardening.

I can talk earthquake statistics or whether her nigella plant survived the trip to my garden. I feel large and useless.

When I hear noises in the kitchen I remember that Bruce comes in each day to prepare their dinner. He is an important difference in Molly's life for she is admitting that at age eighty-five it is comforting to let someone else bustle around in her kitchen, drive her precious 1965 Plymouth Fury, try to tempt Harry with a new food. Her abdication of duty informs her family that she is not expecting to become less sick, or more well. She has installed herself in a somber valley and we must accept the blessed permanence of Bruce, if he will oblige. Harry doesn't accept. He picks at the food on his plate, sniffs the mixed salad hoping to discover that the dressing is laced with more garlic than is allowed, is offended by petrale sole in my honor. "Oh God NO! Not fish!" he says and Bruce says: "Fish it is. Good for you."

I try to recall the crisis which brought Bruce into their lives. Was it the large-size tomato can at the supermarket which jumped from the roller-shelf system and attacked Molly's leg, leaving her bleeding in the aisle? Did Molly study her diary one day and discover that she was getting up at noon, taking a nap from two to five, and retiring at seven-thirty? Or was it her beloved garden, now abandoned to weed and snail?

I feel uneasy that I do not know how much time my sister Anne gives to the household each week. She does not complain to me. It is accepted by everyone that my time is valuable because I say it is even if I'm lolling around reading novels. Yet they say I'm selfish. I pluck the arrow from my chest and flee with the time my selfishness gives me. Anne said to me once in a letter which traveled three thousand miles:

> . . . my feeling towards you doesn't include any shoulds. I am totally uncritical and I don't stop to think about why I am so. Molly says that the first word you spoke was no. I don't know what word I first spoke, but my image of myself in childhood is of compliance and eagerness to please. The opposite of no. You say no to the conventions, no to social requirements, no even to the Law. Contrary, brave, stubborn. Whatever adjective I affix, I envy this quality so much I want to cry when I think of it . . .

Anne and I have been nervously waiting for something further to happen. Something which will let the air out faster. One day in early May, she telephones. She says: "Hello sweetie . . ." There is a hesitation, unusual in a woman who uses the telephone at least half of every day in her job and in any case is not one to call for no reason. The silence tells me what's up, but I ask anyway. "What's up? Did something happen to Molly?"

She sighs, always her prelude to unpleasant news. When Emily tells me something bad, she starts right in on it as soon as I answer the phone. "Guess what, Mom. I have a cyst on an ovary." I prefer Emily's style.

"Well, last week—the day after you left—Harry fell on the way out of the bathroom, *while* pulling up his pants. He either fell or had a slight stroke. He couldn't get up, and to make a long story short . . ."

"Why don't you make it a long story? I have a feeling I'll have to know the facts."

"Oh all right. He lay there on the hall floor vomiting and having a BM and moaning. I called his doctor but he was away on vacation. Then I called the hospital and got no answer! Unbelievable! So I called the police and they said they'd be right over. They brought the Fire Department and it was like TV. They tested and probed and summoned an ambulance on little machines they carry with them. Molly and I followed in the car. Well anyway, he fell in the morning, and at *midnight*, after all the tests and hours of delay, they could find nothing wrong so they sent him home by ambulance."

"And can he walk? Was it a stroke?"

"No, he can't walk and is in a lot of pain." His fault somehow.

"But Molly is not strong enough to take care of him. She scarcely gets from room to room."

"I *know* that. Let me finish, there's more." The irritation is mounting and I concentrate on watching a huge bumble bee climb up the window next to the couch where I sit. "On Friday, I spent the whole damn morning on the telephone trying to get someone to come in during the day so I could go to work, *and* cleaning up the stench and mess Harry left, and I never did get to work. I spent the night there and on Saturday I went to the office for a few hours and while I was gone *Molly* fell!"

"Oh damn! Is she okay?"

"She was outside lying in the driveway when I drove up around four and she'd been there God knows how long, yelling for help because *she* couldn't get up and did something to her hip and broke her glasses *and* her hearing aid."

I feel nervous laughter rising from my stomach. Now on the window ledge a tiny ant is trying to haul up a dead sowbug . . . up, up . . . oops, dropped it. He walks around the body and starts pulling again.

"So the man next door carried her into the house and put her on the couch. More calls. The hospital sent an ambulance and Emily stayed with Harry and more waiting and tests and nothing found and back home again to her bed."

"Why didn't you call me? I could have driven . . ."

"I don't *know* why I didn't."

"When do you want me to come? Today? Tomorrow? When? Is Harry being awful?"

"No. I have to say he's not. Since his fall, there are two differences in him. He won't or can't, I don't know which, stand up. The second difference is that he's not irritable or nasty. He's apologetic for being so helpless, very sweet if anyone peeks in on him, always says please and thank you and oh you are so kind."

"Evidence right there that he's had something afflict his brain, eh?"

"You might say so." We share a little laugh, remembering. "Last night, I was so tired and I *couldn't* get to sleep because he was moaning in his room. It was three o'clock, and I marched downstairs and shouted at him. 'Harry!' I said. 'I cannot get to sleep because you are moaning! You are *going* to take this codeine and SHUT UP! *And* I'm going to close the door!' and do you know what he said?"

"I give up. What did he say?"

"He said: 'Oh, I didn't realize I was moaning. Oh, I am sorry. You go get some sleep, *poor dear Anne!*' I almost dropped the glass of water I was holding and when I got back into bed I couldn't sleep because I couldn't remember any other time in my life that he'd said anything nice to me and I hated . . ."

Anne is in a "state"—as Harry once said of himself. He told his reading public: "Don't tell me I'm in a STATE. I know I am, but I don't want to be told about it." His readers loved his beguiling honesty and envied the family lucky enough to live close to him. I used to wonder how difficult it would be to slip into the composing room and insert my own version of Harry—that restless, inquiring, fretful, irritable, acrid, nasty, dishonest, coughing, sneezing (forty in a sequence), sentimental, talky, balky, mulish father who always came home at night and paid his bills on time. His fans might enjoy hearing that he washed his beautiful hair once a year and it no doubt remained on his head by means of a scalp-glue composed of sweat, dandruff, sediment from San Francisco's busy skies, and nicotine wastes. I know Anne is in a state because she cannot remember that Harry has said many "nice things" about her, has in fact admired and loved her, has bragged about her accomplishments 90 percent of the time since her birth fifty-eight years ago. He's a talented man and just how clever he is can be seen in the power of his 10 percent cruelty. The hurt comes from knowing that the only humility he's ever been known to express has been offered to his readers, for Art. Know, dear Reader, that I am flawed.

"Could you come on Monday?"

"Yes," I say, hoping I can leave Tuesday afternoon.

MOLLY AND HARRY live on a quiet street in Berkeley. The street seems burdened with growth in front gardens, and the trees next to the sidewalk by mid-summer will have grown a ceiling of bright green leaves over all passing cars. There's a four-way stop a few feet from their driveway and seven Asian-American boys are playing softball. They pause to let me pass and stare after me when I turn left just beyond the flowering mayflower tree. Perhaps I should issue a medical bulletin. But they're just kids, interested in places where ambulances arrive and depart.

I reach into the backseat to collect my green suitcase, purse, straw satchel containing books I might read, journal I might write in, and the grocery bag with red snapper, green chili, fortune cookies, and fresh croissants. I place everything in the driveway and wish I could reverse direction. The croissants are for tomorrow's breakfast instead of, not in addition to, oatmeal or soft-boiled eggs. My theory is that when you're sick, you need something to remind you that life contains more than what's good for you. The fortune cookies are for me, messages from outside the stopped time I'm entering.

The front door is unlocked and when I step inside, I am aware of silence, a crowded hush like a Japanese paper flower which does not open until you float it on water. Lacking some necessary element, the house waits, has been waiting since Harry's retirement. For twenty years, Molly has had her volatile husband with her every day to help with gardening tasks and the waxing of wooden floors. With her fretful encouragement, he has written two books which publishers returned to him with kind notes suggesting that there was no demand for an update on Strunk's *Elements of Style* and bewailing the lack of reader interest in California labor history. And in any case, the Sales Department wondered if at age seventy, Harry could be considered a "property" with much future. He could understand their point of view, couldn't he? Last week Bruce told me my father sat on a stool in the kitchen and said: "I couldn't sleep last night because of the pain."

"How do you feel now?" Bruce asked.

"I feel fine because I took a codeine."

"Why don't you go take a nap before dinner?"

"Because I want to stay awake to enjoy the absence of pain."

"Oh, yes, of course, enjoying the absence of something. Interesting."

I place my suitcase and straw bag beside the couch and pause a moment to listen to water splashing in the kitchen.

"HELLO EVERYBODY!" I shout. There is no answer. I walk resolutely into the kitchen with the groceries.

"Hi, Bruce!"

"Hello, Candida. Nice to see you."

"I bought red snapper for dinner. I know Harry doesn't like fish but I think Red Snapper à la Vera Cruz might tempt him. There's a recipe here somewhere. I typed it out last week and I'll prepare it, if you're too busy."

"No problem. I can do it if you'll guide me, and I might as well learn it now as later. I think your mother is . . . well . . . she was visiting your father a while ago."

I enter the dark hallway leading to Molly's bedroom on the left and Harry's on the right. Molly visiting Harry? She's walking? In Harry's doorway she is hunched over an aluminum walker. Long stringy gray hair hangs down over a chest which curves inward towards a back hump. She is wearing a rumpled pink nightgown partially hidden from view by a quilted pink bed-jacket with mid-length sleeves. Her long brown fingers, grasping the rubber supports, are trembling with the effort needed for the next tiny forward movement. She pauses to rest and slowly turns her head to look back into the dark of Harry's bedroom.

"Goodbye, my dear one . . ."

"Goodbye, dear heart."

I am afraid to startle her with a greeting, and knowing my feet want to retreat, I consider returning to the kitchen until she has reached her bedroom. I can't believe she can complete the journey. I step forward until I stand next to the walker. The top of her head is level with my waist. How do I shrink enough to greet her?

"Molly? MOLLY?" This creature is too small, too old, older than old women in photographs on museum walls, with light effects emphasizing the stretching of skin over bone. The face below me lifts towards the sound. She smiles.

"Oh Can'da, I didn't know you were here."

My mother is not wearing her hearing aid or her glasses. Or her teeth. Her hair is not even tied back with the pink velvet ribbon I know is her favorite.

"Harry! Can'da is here."

"MOLLY! ARE YOU HEADED FOR BED? MAY I HELP?"

I ask. But how? I cannot push, or pull, or lift her ninety pounds. Any action seems dangerous. She could fall forward or backward or down.

"No . . . I think I can get there. I'll call you when I need help sitting on the bed. I can't get up or down. It's a mess, isn't it? Go say hello to Harry."

I slip into Harry's dusky bedroom and hesitate before approaching his bed. To give him time to see if he can see me. To hear my "Hello, Harry." Time to decide if I will kiss—not an automatic gesture in this family. He lifts his head and shades his watery eyes with one misshapen hand.

"Anne? Who? Candida! How good of you to come!"

I lurch forward and hide my confusion with a kiss. He lifts his chin and the stubble cuts into my face. His dry hand squeezes my cool fingers and I back away again, uncertain what to say or do. While I stare at him, I chatter about my drive through the Santa Cruz mountains and he tells me which roads he walked to get from Watsonville to Soquel, when he was nine. His head has lost its breadth, and its length from the white hair on top, peaked from lying so long on a pillow, to gray chin hairs pushing out, is excessive. His red, stick-out ears have receded into his skull and he is not wearing his teeth. His cheeks fall inward and I check with my tongue inside my mouth to see how far it is from one side to the other. He is wearing a black-banded wristwatch which looks too heavy for his thin white wrist. The shades are down to protect his hurting eyes. The TV set is dark and silent in front of a window which might look out on the lovely back garden if . . . why can't Harry de-function all at once like the wonderful one-hoss shay he used to recite from memory?

"So, you had a fall. Can you stand up or walk?"

"No. I'm not ready to do that. I have to rest for a while." He sinks down into the pillow.

"How long is a while?"

I pick up the white porcelain bedpan on the chair beside his bed and empty the yellow liquid into the toilet adjoining his bedroom. There's an unpleasant odor of Pine-Sol mixed with his scalp smell, musty sheets, and the air-less musk I have always associated with his sleeping rooms. Wherever they have lived, Molly and Harry have always had separate bedrooms and an extra writing room for Harry. The den did not smell anything like the room in which he slept, and when they made love, Harry went to Molly's fresh, sweet-smelling double-bed, and not the other way around. I don't know how I know this. Certainly I never saw him emerge at dawn, or enter at midnight and close the door behind him.

"I don't know how long a while is. I think I had a fall. I don't remember. And I don't know where this room is, or where Molly's room is, or even where the house is . . . on what street or land. When Bruce brings my food, I can't visualize where he came from . . . where the kitchen is."

He looks sweetly puzzled. The sweet part is new and never-before. It now bubbles up from deep inside the ruined body, not planned or under his control. Although I have never talked with this new-old man before, I accept the change as permanent and am fairly sure I'll never battle with him again.

"Does it bother you that you don't remember? Do you want me to describe the house?"

"It doesn't bother me, it interests me, the loss, and yes, thank you, I'd like you to tell me what happened and where I am." He turns over onto his back slowly and says: "Oh Christ! What a nuisance!" Not asking me for sympathy. I wait for his pain to subside. I'd like to comfort him but when he turns his face towards me again, I lock my hands behind my back and perch on the edge of his TV stand.

"What's a nuisance, Harry?"

"Existence is a nuisance. Remembering where I am. Eating. Sleeping. All of it, a damn nuisance." Not angry or petulant. Not Job (a favorite of his). Sweet, weary resignation. He rests his thin head on a hill of pillows. He lifts his bony wrist and squints at the tiny numbers on his watch. His arm falls to the sheet.

"Can'da! Please . . . I can't seem to . . ." From far, far away I hear Molly's raspy cry.

"Molly's calling. I'll be back later."

"Turn out the light. I mean . . . turn the light on in the bathroom and turn out the light here beside my bed."

"No you don't. Bruce's fixing dinner. Red snapper. You have to eat before you say goodnight."

"Oh yes, I forgot. Red snapper. Good. I like fish. Now. Thank you for coming to see me. What time is it?"

"It's five-forty-five."

I hurry across the hall to Molly's bedroom. She is standing beside her bed, hunched over her walker. She peeks through the long, uncombed strands of thin gray hair. I reach out my arms to help but don't know where to put them. She must tell me what to do.

"I can't let go. It hurts too much. Only a damn few inches, but I can't do it. Just support me under the arms. Your back, Can'da . . . can you do it?"

"My back's fine. Okay, now you can let go. I have you."

I stand in front of her and place my hands in her armpits. My fingers feel bone and I'm afraid they'll poke through the paper-skin and emerge beneath her ears. She sinks to the bed and her pink granny-gown hikes up over rice-paper knees, knobby like bleached gingerroot. She now has the slender legs she always wanted. She sits on the edge of the bed, her long fingers resting on the mattress edge. She lifts one hand and reaches for her hearing aid on her bedside stand. I'm afraid she'll fall forward.

"NEVER MIND THE AID. YOU CAN PUT IT IN LATER." I remember to speak loudly. Her hand returns to the mattress.

"Obscenity! Old age is an obscenity! There should be some way to get rid of us!" She looks into my face and dares me to disagree. She's right, but only last week the tiny bit of gardening she was able to do, her journal, a visit from Anne, planning a menu, feeding the mockingbird, sitting at twilight with Mamacat in her lap, eating her seed bread, reading, reading—these events were almost enough for her. Words of encouragement jam in my throat. She has the means. Pills on her bedside stand, prescription sleeping pills, codeine for pain. Each capsule that helps her to stay can also allow her to leave. I can't even clear my throat to tell her she is dear to me. I fluff up the pillows and wait for her to pull herself back onto the bed.

"My dear, I can't lift my legs. If you could . . ."

"Oh, I didn't know." I lift the stalks carefully. They have little weight. "Just let yourself down . . . on my arms."

"Turn me . . . off my hip. It hurts."

I scoop beneath her buttocks. I feel bone and a lump the size of a softball. "What's that? That lump!"

"Where I fell."

"May I look?" She nods and gazes out the window. I lift the pink gown and am astonished that so small a woman could produce so huge a manifestation of a body's fight. Intense purplish-red in color, it looks alive, as though it could move around at will. I cover her with a sheet and blanket and feel dizzy. I remove a pile of *Organic Gardening* from the rocking chair and sit down, feeling trapped in the antique chair, in the room, the pain, disease, decay, the clutter of abandoned tasks. Garters to be attached to corsets on top of the sewing machine, stockings to be mended. The closed journal lying beneath her right hand (*Journal: 1980* in gold lettering). A packet of unpaid bills wrapped with a rubber band and labeled "Bills" in Anne's handwriting. Magazines, newspapers, books piled at the foot of the bed. She's brought her life into this room, reduced, almost manageable. Even Mamacat can enter, through the window, if someone will open it. Only Harry, her dear heart, remains outside because he can't or won't get out of bed and walk across the hall.

And I've noticed already that, although the hall is straight and one can go left into Molly's room or right into Harry's, the light curves towards Molly's effort, and I've almost forgotten that a man lies alone in the almost-dark with no object, not even a book face down on the bed, to remind him of a task unfinished. His den with twelve dictionaries is in a part of the house he can't remember. He also can't remember his snug workroom with entry door on the garden side of the house, where each tool has its place, where an easy chair is jammed in between an old-fashioned radio and a carpenter's workbench, daily newspapers piled neatly beneath. Harry made wooden boxes, dollhouses, furniture, cutting boards, bookcases, plant stands, shelves, and footstools. Those items his children or grandchildren refused are piled to the ceiling in his toolroom.

"What time is it, dear?" Molly is wearing her wristwatch, but in order to see her wrist she would first have to lift an arm and without her glasses, find her glasses. She might be able to read the numbers on the digital clock-radio, but to do that she'd have to turn her head. They both want to know the time. Why? I don't wear a watch, preferring not to know directly what I can learn so easily—the dog pestering for her food at five o'clock each day, the flutter of birds at sundown, traffic sounds at seven-thirty in the morning and again at five.

"It's five-fifty-five and Bruce is almost ready with dinner. Just lie back and I'll give you your glasses and your hearing aid." My voice is not loud.

"I can't lie back." But she crumples into the pillow, closes her eyes, tears wetting the dry cheeks. I adjust her covers and place her glasses on her nose. She loops the plastic crescents over her ears with two crooked fingers of her left hand. I put her hearing aid into her hand.

"I don't want to put it on," she whispers. I would like to comb her hair for her but her head lies now on a pillow and my caring about the snarls and the look of a woman's crowning glory might seem a reproof. I linger at her bedside and wonder if Molly is deciding which means, which day, what words to leave behind.

AFTER DINNER, I collect two trays from two beds. Molly is asleep but looks dead. Her head has rolled into a cavern between two pillows, and her mouth (without teeth) is open. Harry has tucked himself around his tray and has spilled his salad onto his blanket. His mouth (without teeth) is open. I wash the dishes by hand. I don't know how to work the dishwasher and find I'm grateful for this. There is no rack for drying and so I dry each dish and glass, searching through the cupboards for the proper place for a small bowl or a Chinese plate with jade-green center, and I stretch all the rubber-bands between the knobs, there to keep the dishes in their piles in the event of an earthquake finally coming to this house.

I wander into the living room, pick up a magazine, but don't want to read about farm workers or what to do if your rosebush has leaves with holes, and everywhere I sit I feel I'm sitting on a mother or father. There is a dinner hour in this household. Is there a time for saying goodnight? I draw the drapes, lock the front door, turn on the porch light, and listen for sounds from the bedrooms.

"Can'da . . . Can'da . . . are you there?" Molly calls me from far away. I stand at the door of her room. Again I stare at the deep hollows of her eyes, the cheekbones with stretched shiny skin, the skull behind her ears, supported by the tiny neck. She is aware of my concern, knows what I fear for myself and would like to hide her body in deep fertile earth forever. I must look only at the brown eyes and listen to the woman in shadow behind them.

"I have made a decision and I don't want any argument from you." She wrinkles her nose and squinches her face at me. "There's a little box in my closet. Can you get it, dear? It's on my dresser. Yes that's it."

Resting on cotton inside a blue box is her engagement ring, old-gold with a diamond set in raised cobweb-gold tracery. I offer it to her.

"I'm giving it to Emily. I want her to have it *now*. My finger has drawn away from it and it falls off. There's no sense at all in burying it with me. She doesn't want to accept and she won't say what she wants in the house, and you won't and Anne gets cross."

"EMILY WILL LOVE THE RING AND TREASURE IT BECAUSE IT IS YOURS," I shout, and wonder if my words come to her ears like a muffled roar and can she translate them into the caress which is intended?

Candida's yelling, has to yell so Molly can hear, but there's nothing wrong with my ears. I hear everything they say to her. All the people who come into my room and then leave me and go to her. Always her. Leave me as fast as they can. They hope I'm dying. They hope. They try to get me up but they don't want me up. I know I'm dying and I don't care about that. Just going to take a long time doing it. Want to remember a few things first. It's hard to remember. On mourra seul . . . Quid est, Catulle? I can remember better than all of them. Can't remember the unimportant things. They do that, always have. Molly wants to give away my engagement ring. Maybe she'll tell me about it and she'll want me to get upset but I'll just not hear her. And she wants me to eat fish because Candida says it's healthy food, as though there is health out there to be had. They think I'm sweet because I've had a stroke. It's just to fool them. Anne is especially funny when I act so humble and appreciate what she does for me. She doesn't know how to act. Doesn't know where to put her habit of hating me. That Candida, she's not fooled. She observes and plans on writing it down. Her being here with us and how we look, all of it. But she'll never sell a damn thing. Stuff lacks significance. Doesn't know the language. I was a better writer at twenty than she is at . . . I don't know how old she is. Selfish always. Children! Yea, Carnage is thy Daughter, the children born of thee are sword and fire, Red Ruin, and the breaking up of laws. Terrible poet, Tennyson. Or was it? Whoever it was I remember the lines, remember the important things. She's here now hoping I'll go to sleep. I'll be so sweet her heart will turn, but she will not soften. Just the light out and the pan near. That's all she has to do. I'm no trouble now. Not really.

The next morning the amplified bell rings at eight.

"You mus' be Candida. I'm Eula." Eula is immense. When she leans over to set down her satchel we are the same height. "How's Mr. and Mrs. Gavin? Have they had breakfast yet? Today is Mrs. Gavin's day for a bath an' bed change for both of them. I'm real glad you're here 'cause you can help with the bath. Don' want no one to fall. You got y'dog here? I like dogs. I'm not 'fraid. Jes' want to know so's I won' be s'prised when I open the back door."

"No. I left her in a kennel."

"Yeah. They's cat people. Cat people get nerves when dogs is around. An' the dogs, they know it. Not me. I like dogs."

I follow her down the hall to Molly's room.

"G'MORNIN', MRS. GAVIN! HOW YOU THIS MORNIN'?" she says to the face on the pillow, to the open mouth which looks like a hole in cracked adobe. I peer around Eula's pale blue nylon shoulder to see Molly's mouth slowly closing, swallowing the hole. I don't want to watch Molly return to her body and feel I lack a training that Eula exudes like a highway patrol officer. I'm wearing pajamas, haven't washed my face or brushed my teeth, haven't had breakfast. I'm clearly disadvantaged and must hurry to catch up to Eula's corporeal, perhaps spiritual, headstart.

I duck into the bathroom and lock the door, remove a plastic bench from the bathtub floor and uncoil a long spray attachment looped around the shower head. When I turn on the water I am sprayed in the face with cold water which splatters into the toilet behind me. I adjust knobs until my pajamas are wet. The knobs are as sharp as cactus and the cold water is on the left. Is that where it usually is? There's no "C" or "H" and the right-hand knob turns off in a clockwise direction, the left-hand knob counterclockwise.

This seems odd. I adjust the spray to a suitable temperature and force, and climb over the side into the tub. I aim the water at my face and reach for the soap. Suddenly the water temperature plummets to freezing; in panic I throw the damn gadget onto the tub floor and step high over the side to safety. I wonder, not for the first time, why plumbing manufacturers are trying to kill customers. I feel sure Harry arranged these bath eccentricities. Did Molly complain? Or did she adjust herself rather than risk a fight?

When I emerge from the bathroom, I am dressed in turtleneck and jeans for whatever "work" will be required of me. Eula is reading at the kitchen table. She looks up at me and smiles. "Your mother and father's eatin'. It take a long time for ol' folks t'eat. Mrs. Gavin wants to wait 'til afternoon for her bath. She say she too tired an' weak an' want to talk with you."

I hold in my hand a slice of Molly's seed bread and look for a pop-up toaster. On the counter there's a toaster oven. "Eula, I lead a very simple life. I don't have conveniences in my kitchen. Matter of fact, I don't even have a kitchen. I don't know how to work the dishwasher or the washing machine, that model anyway. How do I toast this piece of bread?"

"Oh, woman! You jes' put the bread in that oven an' push the lever down an' wait." She rises up huge and competent and places my bread in the oven, closes the little door and pushes down the red lever. She laughs kindly at my confusion.

"This kitchen is beyond me. I'm going to run around the block as soon as I finish breakfast." I lurch around the room being nervously silly.

"My doctor, he say I mustn't run, but I got to do thirty minutes of ex'cises ev'ry day to get this flab off my stomach." She lifts her uniform top to show me dark-brown luscious rolls of fat. The skin is taut over excess, without vein or white streak. "It look like beer done that to me, but I can't 'bide alcohol. My husband, he drink two six-pack a day, after work. He's . . . I'm not s'posed to talk about family while I'm on the job. Sound like your toast is ready."

She sits down again at the kitchen table where she's reading sheets of paper each with a black cross printed in top-left corner.

"What're you reading, Eula? Doesn't look like anything you found in this house."

She smiles up at me. "This house got hidden love in it. Tha's all that matter. I have body ex'cises and spirit ex'cises. Thirty minutes a day of each kind. I'm doin' my spirit ex'cises. I don' need these papers. I can do it in my head while I work. This is Matthew Chapter 5 an' I already know all the Blesseds by heart. Seem like I always knew them. But I like to read 'em, seein' what's in your insides right out there on the table."

"Blessed are those who eat seed bread and drink weak coffee in the House of their parents. Is that it?"

"Oh you like to make a joke, jes' like your father. Your mother, she don' make too many jokes, not now anyway."

I mix my coffee with half and half and spread butter on the seed bread. Why can't I leave Eula intact? Why does this family resent simple faith, brood about God's place in the lives of others, and feel especially skittish and mean when sharing space with Divine Guidance? We should post "Thou Shalt Not Worship" signs on the walls, on the front door, and see then who walks past the warning to clean the urine smell from draining bodies.

I STOP OUTSIDE MOLLY'S BEDROOM and listen for a sound from Harry's side of the hall. Nothing. The tiny headboard light on Molly's bed is on but the shades are down. Eula has drawn back the drapes in the living room and has told me it is a sunny day on the outside. So, who doesn't know that? Mamacat is crying on the car-port roof. Molly is asleep, her head placed at an awkward angle on the pillow. I feel a runaway itch in my feet as I stand in the hallway, almost a pain moving up to my ankles. Molly cannot begin her day. I must do it for her. My release will come after beginning, but what if she will not even let in the cat or notice that the sun is shining? Will I then become a fixed, unmoving part of the silence which surrounds me? I stare at the breakfast tray, searching for signs that something has happened since Eula said good morning to Molly. The paper napkin is crumpled and there is a piece of carefully cut cantaloupe dislodged from its rind. One bite (or is it only a torn edge?) is missing from the slice of bread. I step forward into her room. I don't want to see her mouth close, must show her the sun, warm her, myself. I raise the shades and open the window to let in Mamacat. She's a nervous cat. She meows at me, but ducks under my caress and turns from me to knead Molly's chest, her tail flicking and curling. Can I learn from her decisive style? Molly's hand brushes against mine as we stroke the arched back, warm still from morning sun. My left hand presses down on scattered newspapers, rustling them. Mamacat leaps from the bed, like a bird lifting off carrion.

"Oh Candida! I hurt everywhere. Everywhere. What is the sense? I can't go on. I won't." I lift the tray and place it on the top of her cluttered bureau. I lean over her and try to plump her pillows. Her 1980 white and gold diary lies next to her pillow. A stained and ragged square of sheet covers the bedspread. I want to remove it and make her bed a pretty place.

"Never mind. It doesn't matter. Did you sleep well?"

"YES. YES. VERY WELL," I shout. Unusually well. My last thought, I remember, was that Harry couldn't climb the stairs to the bedroom to ask if I needed an extra blanket, or a book, or to show me how to open a window.

She rolls onto her right elbow. I perch on the side of the bed, newspapers beneath me. "Candida, the man next door, the man who carried me into the house, he's a Jew, did you know that?" I want to laugh, but Molly is very serious. I nod my head: yes, I knew. I shrug my shoulders: so what? "He carried me. It was very nice of him, but I saw his eyes, big, dark pools of fear. He knew that I knew that he was a Jew, and how terrible that all of them have to fear! Terrible! That fear. That I would not want him to touch me, that I would be angry. Awful! What a world!" She sinks down again into her pile of pillows.

"Molly, I don't think . . ."

"Never mind! I know what he felt." She stares out the window at the branch that arches from his yard over onto the carport. I study the tangle of Molly's words. I see myself ringing his doorbell and when he answers I say I'm sorry and walk dejectedly back down the flower border to the sidewalk, then take my place at bedside, where I await the next news. It isn't the first time. Somewhere in my files I have a "Molly's Crazy Ideas" list. Categories, subcategories, quotations. Anne said once, long ago: "I can't stand it when she says *anything* about Jews! I can't fit it in or make sense of it. It's dirty and crazy."

Upset by my sister's distress, I tried to soothe: "I block it. I shake my head and it seems to drop down into a void along with · her belief in earthquake weather and her suspicion of all female friendships. If it helps any, I don't believe she's dangerous."

Molly's mournful eyes are staring at me. "Did you read about Mono Lake sinking so low that all the predators can just walk out and eat the birds? *What* is happening to our world?"

"TERRIBLE, MOLLY, TERRIBLE! DID YOU WRITE IT IN YOUR DIARY?"

She places her hand on the white and gold book. "No, it's finished."

"MOLLY! I'M GOING FOR A WALK. I'LL BE BACK FOR YOUR BATH."

"Yes dear, but be careful."

She wants to get away from this house, from me, from Harry. Seems to me she has always wanted that. She is so selfish. I wonder why she is here now, what Anne told her about us. That we are dying? Is dying a reason to visit us? She doesn't want any of our beautiful things. Well, she won't get even a stick. She would have a garage sale and sell everything. Eula, a black woman, cares more for us. She gets paid but she would care anyway. Candida and Anne, they'd rather we hire, spend our money, our precious money. Well good. We'll spend it all outside the family until there's nothing left for them. She's so selfish. Doesn't care about the decay in our environment. Doesn't wash apples. That's why she got cancer. Eats fish. Thinks fish is safe. No, she didn't say that. She doesn't care, she just likes fish. Always so fiercely judgmental. Wonder how she got that way? Harry and I, always liberal, tolerant. She just walks away from lives that don't amuse her, says she hasn't time, or is bored. She'll be old soon. Fish and exercise won't prevent what has happened to me. She's had cancer and she'll get it again. I notice that her middle finger is swollen—arthritis. She won't admit it, but I know. I wonder if Harry is dead in his bedroom. I can't get up to see. Eula wouldn't let that happen. Sometimes I wish he would die. I hate his groans and smells. His room. He is unclean, always has been. He is so cruel to me. But I do love him, he is my dear husband.

Bath time for Molly. We've been leading up to it since eight a.m. It is now two in the afternoon. Eula is apprehensive about falls and blackouts and she assures me that she would not attempt a bath if I were not here. She looks strong enough to pick up my little mother. Surely she can prevent a precipitous drop. She says: "Your mama's jes' a little thing in her body, but she's huge with dignity. Jes' huge! She's goin' to walk from her bed to the bath, and tha's about ten miles for you or me, an she won' have it any other way. This is the Trial an' if she kin do it, she'll be better tomorrow. Ol' folks have their pride an' dignity an' tha's what worries me about Mr. Gavin. His laziness, jes' lost his dignity. He don' want to get it back. Jes' want to go downhill, codeine and more codeine an' sleep an' pee in his bed an' forgit where his slippers is. His bein' so unnatural sweet, he's thinkin' tha's goin' to get him care an' lovin' but when he get a little better, he's goin' to get a su'prise or two. He like to eat. Eats three meals a day and want more. He's goin' to find out that food has no feet. Tha's what his feet're for, to walk to the food, all prepared nice for him an' set on the table. OKAY MRS. GAVIN! ALL

READY FOR THE BATH? LET'S TAKE OFF THAT WATCH. YOU WANT YOUR GLASSES ON?"

Molly is sitting on the side of the bed, her legs hanging down, swollen blue ankles, the big feet idle, curving towards each other. She lifts her arm to Eula and while the close-cropped dark head is bent over her wrist, she gazes at me, her eyes reproaching me, seeming to accuse me of inventing Existence, her existence on the edge of a bed. Her stained pink bathrobe is open down the front and she's showing me, indifferent, the body I came from, will become.

"MRS. GAVIN, YOU WANT YOUR GLASSES ON?"

Molly looks at Eula. She's not wearing her hearing aid, but she hears, slowly. "Yes. Of course I want my glasses on. I can't see without them."

"OKAY MRS. GAVIN, ARE YOU GOIN' TO WALK WITH YOUR WALKER? OR DO YOU WANT US TO BE YOUR WALKER?"

"I want to use my walker. It will take a long time, but yes, I want to do that. I can do that."

I set the walker in front of her knees. Eula and I stand at attention, a soldier on each side of the veteran. Life must be respected. Effort. If she walks to the bath she does not want, she has dignity. If we carry her, she will appear to lack a quality the old must keep until they die. Molly wants to die. She has said so. She has always wanted to die and has passed the wish to me. Genetic. A shadowing behind my eyes which is visible to anyone who can see, like the yellow of jaundice. The rugs, the antiques, the Chinese bowls, the money in the bank—these are not my inheritance. How puzzled the doctor was when I woke up with my breast gone and told him he had no right, he had no right! I wanted to think about death and choose. People don't like to think of death. They say they never do, it's morbid. Molly's breasts, she doesn't hide them now. She lets them show through her robe. Sacks, empty and hanging, the color of dust, no color in the nipples, catching in the folds of her stomach. A part of her she's forgotten.

"THA'S RIGHT, MRS. GAVIN. YOU'RE DOIN' FINE! YOU'LL GET THERE!"

"I hurt! Obscene. There should be a way to get rid of me. Of us. Don't listen to me. Oh you are both so good . . . thank . . . I don't think . . ."

"YES YOU CAN. YOU'RE JUST FINE. DON' WORRY. WE'VE GOT YOU."

I can look up at Eula's brown neck, at the ear decorated with a shiny large pearl, the expanse of poreless dark skin, that cap of frizzy hair, the smile, white and serene. Or down at Molly's enormous head held rigid, the greasy strands of hair clinging to her shoulders, the hump—oddly appealing—the flexed long fingers protruding above the aluminum handles, the callused, scaly toes inching forward, first one, then the other.

· · ·

EULA IS WEARING HER NURSE'S WATCH and she tells me, softly, when we arrive at the side of the bathtub, that it took Molly twenty-five minutes to make the journey.

"Let me sit. I am tired. Weary."

"RIGHT HERE, MRS. GAVIN. YOU'RE DOIN' FINE!"

She is standing in front of the toilet. I lower the lid.

"No . . . no . . . lift the lid." The mistake was to forget that she might want to pee. She is incontinent, she says of herself. She offers self-disgust which she dares me to share. She cannot contain her waters. And when I tell her that a small operation could repair, she says she does not want to be repaired, doesn't want me to mop up the yellow leak or pick up the soggy rags from the floor, says Eula can do it. I want to clean and mop and serve food, want to do what Eula does. I am not a symbol left behind to mark the trail.

Eula and I hear the soft plop of matter hitting water. There is no smell. We smile at each other, pleased that we have provided the conditions in which Molly can perform a natural act. We are very tall, high above Molly's head. While she fastidiously wipes, Eula turns on the spray and adjusts knobs. Molly tries to reach behind to push down the flusher. She fails and tears drip below the steamed glasses. I push the knob for her and she clutches her hands together over her stomach.

"I THINK WE'RE READY NOW, MRS. GAVIN. LEMME TAKE YOUR GLASSES. THAT OL' SPRAY IS A DEVIL AN' WE'LL JUST GET YOU IN AN' ADJUST IT AGAIN."

Eula, her solid body wedged now between toilet and opaqued window, leans forward to offer a hand to Molly. An arm circles beneath the tangled hair. I grip Molly's wedding hand. I feel the effort in my body, the trite strength of my legs and back.

"Ridiculous. I can't . . . can't do it. I can't get off this toilet. Oh dear." She sends me a hollow I-am-sorry stare which enters me. I sat there—when was it?—and looked up at her—not here— not in this room.

"Candida, put your hand under her arm. Tha's right. OKAY MRS. GAVIN. WE HAVE YOU NOW. UP YOU GO. Careful. Blackouts come when you change position." We have raised Molly to a standing posture. She stands at the river. Her robe falls to the floor without our help.

"Throw that over in the corner so she don' trip on it." I am eager to obey Eula, who seems healthy and normal, is the right color, and knows what to do next. Molly, naked, is wrong. The direction of her skin, for instance. Down, hanging on her bones, like Spanish moss on dead tree limbs. The hump is shiny-white, solid useless desolate sculpture. Veins and skin, intertwining, hanging loose from shoulders, upper arms, neck, thighs, buttocks, knees, assembling at blue feet. The bony scaffold swaying against strong brown arms.

We give Molly one shoulder, one hand each, and Eula has to step into the bathtub to help get the legs over the side. It would be so much easier just to pick up the bones and place them on the bath bench.

"Wouldn't it be easier . . . ?" I mumble.

"Easy get you there, but it don't get you back," Eula says. Why don't I have a supply of maxims which could help me know how to act? Why is it like the first instance in history every time I do anything? Now we have to help Molly lower herself to the bench. She goes down hard on the bones that are her buttocks. Just bones, with skin hanging over the sides of the bathtub seat. Molly has the spray now and is aiming at the place where she cannot contain her waters. My left hand is under her solid hump, my right hand cupped below her armpit, and I'm getting wet. She slips a tiny piece of soap in and out of the lips of skin. There is no hair on her mound, which, without hair, is not a mound. The spray parts the folds of skin. I cannot look away. I am the frame of Molly's old age. When the picture fades and crumbles, I'll be left behind. I tell myself I'm helping Molly take a bath, Eula and I are making it possible for Molly to have dignity.

"DO YOU WANT ME TO WASH YOUR HAIR, MRS. GAVIN?"

"No. I am through washing. I'm tired and cold. And old. We can wash my hair tomorrow." She is looking at the wall in front of her. And yes, she does have dignity, sitting there naked on bones draped with onionskin, smelling like Cashmere-Bouquet, with her two servants at her side.

We wrap Molly in a large pink towel. She can smile now and look into our faces. It takes another hour to get her back in bed and she falls asleep while we are adjusting her pillows. Eula tells me that two and one-half hours have elapsed.

"Now we have to give Mr. Gavin a sponge bath an' change his bed. He's easy. He likes to be babied."

Eula washes all of Harry while I yank blankets and sheets and try to remove all the sources of sour smell. His teeth are floating in a glass of water amidst bits of transparent scum. Feeling sick, I empty the water into the toilet and place the teeth in clean water. They bob up and down. I wait beside the bed. Eula coos and smiles and he says thank you Beulah and oh that feels good and how is Molly? He has lots of hair left though his penis is quite pale and tiny and the sack seems to have lost its contents. The only trouble we encounter is in getting the sleeves of his clean bathrobe over his arthritic right hand. The fingers are spread at an angle which makes smooth entry difficult. I slide my hand up the sleeve and gently twist and pull until the fingers pop out of the cuff. We help him into a chair and with two of us working on the bed, we're finished before he's half through his story about how his only Ambulance Corps war injury was when he got swacked on Angelica wine and dove for his cot but missed and broke his arm.

Decubitus

When Molly and Harry are again walking, Molly—while gardening—falls a second time and remains in bed through the summer months. She tells me falling is an "event," and except for the pain, she's been feeling more cheerful since. The lump on her hip disappears and the only apparent damage is that a slightly older old age settles on her and she needs more codeine to sleep. In October, she can walk again but has to be helped down the back stairs to her garden and once there, her knees tend to crumple and seat her abruptly in a flower bed or in the compost pile outside the gate. Harry seldom leaves the house and worries when he becomes aware that she is not inside, shuffling, tap-tapping her cane, asking if he's eaten his lunch, has taken a shower, or has heard from Anne.

My visits taper off. I write a cheerful letter occasionally and try to remember to telephone every few days. Molly has an amplifier on her telephone and our conversations are conducted without shouts. She always asks about my health, the garden, Jack, and my work. She wants to know that it is going well but doesn't care to hear what I'm writing. She donates twenty-five years of her daily diary and wonders if the volumes are useful. I tell her they are interesting and that I've included portions, but don't say they serve to ground my story in the boring and trivial and in the cutting stage, I shall ruthlessly prune.

Late in October, she says: "When you come in next week, I want you to take me to dinner *without* Harry. He doesn't have to go everywhere I go."

"Isn't that going to cause trouble, mostly for you?"

"I have trouble with him without provoking it. I don't want to discuss it but I do have something I need to talk to you about alone. I don't even want Anne to go. So, that's what we'll do."

When I arrive, shortly before six, there is no Harry slumped over his portable electric heater, lifting his hand to shade his eyes, saying, "So soon? What time is it? Where is Anne? She should be here." I want to greet him and receive permission for the unusual engagement I have with his wife of sixty years. She belongs to him and I feel I am borrowing her without asking. He likes to lend his possessions (excluding his car) but requires recognition that contracts (to whom, under what conditions) have been entered into. When I see that his bedroom door is closed, I wonder if Bruce will find a corpse on the bed after he knocks to announce dinner and no one answers. I even want to comfort him. Leaving him behind at his age, when for better or worse he has always included us, is a serious act and I am sure Molly hasn't thought of tomorrow's consequences (petulance, insults, sulks, shouts).

Molly stands in front of her bureau. She tucks one last wisp of hair under a green velvet ribbon and smiles up at me. "Don't worry about *him*. Bruce will stay to eat dinner and he'll be all right until we get back. Good for him to have a change of routine." She is wearing her dark-green pants suit and the ugly brown Red Cross oxfords I have disliked all my life. (She has four pairs in a row on her closet floor—garden shoes, town shoes, walking shoes, best shoes, tan, brown, dark-brown, and black.) I know what an effort it must have been to bend over and tie the shoelaces and suddenly I want to cuddle her big feet in my hands and ask her to forgive all the annoyance I have felt at having a mother who has always been clean and neat but never stylish, never frivolous.

"Well, I'm ready. We'll have to walk slowly and I hope there are no steps at the restaurant."

"YOU LOOK GOOD! SMELL DELICIOUS!" I shout. While my words echo through the house, I cock my head towards Harry's door and ask Molly in pantomime if she thinks I should greet or ignore. She wrinkles her nose and raises her chin. "Take my arm. I'm afraid of falling on these floors."

She sits stiffly upright in my dirty Datsun and I drive slowly and carefully to the corner restaurant where I know we can order, in casual dignity, a soup or salad (hold the salt), with no one rushing about. When I turn off the ignition, she puts her hand on my arm and says: "This is a nice car. Just the right size. Mine is too big even though I love it because my dear sister gave it to me."

"It's a very dirty car, but gets amazing mpg."

"I can't hear you."

"IT'S A VERY DIRTY . . ."

"Never mind. I've come to a decision. I think Harry and I *must* get a divorce! I can't go on with him any longer and I *deserve* peace and quiet in the time I have left!"

"Oh Molly! Has he . . . HAS HE DONE SOMETHING RECENTLY? SOMETHING UNUSUAL?"

"What is recent is that I've been adding it all up. He is awful, *awful* to me. He thinks I have pain just to annoy him, he gets angry when I can't hear him, he is *brutal* to our dear Anne who visits every day and works so hard at controlling her temper. I have decided I want a place I can see her by myself. She'll find a place. For him or for me." Her wrist, poking forth from the green cuff, is no wider than her cane. I can see a blue vein throbbing in her dry hand.

"SHALL WE GO IN OR WOULD YOU RATHER TALK HERE?"

"Oh, are we there? I'm very hungry."

It takes a long time for Molly to step out of the car and walk across the sidewalk to the restaurant door. She seems to grow smaller and more frail with each step. She drops her cane and says: "Oh dear!" The waitress smiles kindly and seats us in a corner away from kitchen noise. I sit with my back to the patrons so that when I have to shout, my voice will bounce off the window. Molly seems pleased with my choice of restaurant and carefully studies the menu.

"My dear, just order a green salad for me and some good brown bread. I hope Harry is all right but I'm glad he isn't with us. He doesn't know how to behave in restaurants."

I shudder, remembering the Harry-pattern of first abusing the help, then asking about their families while they fidget, and finally thanking each one personally and leaving a big tip. In between, he complains about the food, scolds Molly for being such a fussy eater, tells long stories we've heard before, and drops his napkin on the floor.

"DO YOU CARE IF YOU MOVE FROM YOUR HOUSE? OR DO YOU WANT HARRY TO MOVE?" I glance behind me and am relieved to find all eyes averted.

"Oh dear! I don't care. I can't take care of that house and garden. I want to be alone in a room with Mamacat and a refrigerator. My pots in the window. Someone to look in on me now and then, and Anne visiting. I'm going to read that long architectural study of a monastery. It costs $300 and will take up all the time left. Anne says I might as well buy it."

"WHY ARE YOU CRYING IF YOU'RE SO SURE?" I place my hand over her tiny wrist, not daring to apply pressure.

"My teeth are clacking and I can hear them, but I can't hear you unless you shout. That's why. Harry will be fine staying in the house. That's all he wants to do anyway, just sit and sit. How long will he sit? How long will it be?"

AFTER OUR DINNER, Molly does not again mention getting a divorce. In the weeks before Christmas, she calls me three times, and each time complains of increasing pain, of Harry's failing health and how worried she is about him, and asks the usual questions about my life. One morning she says: "I don't want any Christmas gathering or celebration. Is that all right, dear?"

"Fine by me, you know how I hate the season."

"I feel I must take action before I get any more helpless, while I still can."

"Take action? What do you mean?"

"You *know* what I mean. I know how I'll do it. I can't talk with Anne about it, she is too close to me. Harry says I'm being foolish and screams at me and says he won't listen."

"I'll listen, but I'd rather do it in person. I should be there in a week or two, sooner if you need me. Can you wait?"

"Yes, whenever you can get here. It's very good to talk with you. Goodbye, dear."

I call Anne. "Molly is talking suicide. Has she mentioned it to you?"

"Indirectly. When I press her, she says the family should not know, and then she cries."

"What else does she say?"

"She says she can't go on, shouldn't be required to, she has the means, it's nobody's business."

Molly's second call in December comes at a time when I'm sitting on my couch staring across the room at the telephone. I feel it wants to ring. "Candida! No one will listen to me! I say I am going to do it and they tell me the rains will stop soon, or we'll find a new medicine. The attendants say they'll hear no more such talk, *God* doesn't like it." She is crying, her words wrapped in the rain streaming down my window.

"Dear Molly, I'll listen. You can say anything you want. It's an old subject and we've discussed it before."

"I *know* you'll listen, that's why I'm calling you. Listen is not all I want. I want you to tell me it's . . . sensible, a good solution, that I'm not crazy. Oh, what does it matter if I *am* crazy? *Why* won't people think about it? Why is an old moldy life given such value?"

"Do you want me to answer those questions?"

"No. I want to know who has the right to decide. You *must* tell me what you believe."

"Remember when I wanted to die? You urged me to wait. You said I didn't have the right to leave that legacy to my children. You said things couldn't be worse and might get better. You kept watch over me and urged a faith in the future. Remember?"

"Of course I remember. You were crazy."

"Now I believe that when I become weak and am in pain, with no believable promise of relief, I'll swallow my pills and let people argue the ethical question in my absence. Is that what you want me to say?" I press the receiver hard against my ear. This is what the new humans call "giving permission." I should now be feeling proud of my courage and my victim should be hugging me in a grateful embrace. I see, instead, the rock I have tied to Molly's bare feet and feel my hands pushing her into icy lake waters whose depth no one knows. I feel the struggle to stay alive, that urgent pulse which beat against my fingers when I once tried to drown a defective kitten in the toilet.

"Molly? Molly! I don't want you to die. I want you to stop hurting, that's all."

"It's all right, dear. I feel much better now. You are coming with Louis—my precious grandson—on Christmas day?"

"Yes. We'll stay only a short while. We'll try to get you to go out to dinner and then come back before the freeway crowds. See you then?"

"Yes, my dear."

In the following week, I twice put the dog in the backseat and head for Berkeley, but take an off-ramp five miles up Highway 17 and return home. Inside the house, the telephone and I watch each other. There is a third call two days before Christmas. She inquires about my health, the garden, Jack, and my work. She says Harry is suffering nausea but seems to be responding to a bland diet. Then she asks, in a tone I recognize as Molly's healthy gallows humor: "It would not be *aesthetic* to do it on Christmas Eve, would it?"

"Certainly not! Carolers out in front, presents under the tree. Not aesthetic at all."

She laughs and says Anne will be playing bridge on Christmas day, if I can imagine such a thing, and they'll be waiting for us, don't be too late and drive carefully.

On Christmas Eve, I lie down on my bed but can't sleep. I don't want to prevent my mother's suicide. She is sick and old and no "safe" amount of codeine can make her comfortable. She sometimes asks me if it is okay for her to scream, and when she lets it out, I leave her house. I tell myself I should go there and hold her in my arms. I don't know how to hold her, she has not taught me. Her wrists are too thin, her frame too skeletal, her skull too visible.

At four a.m. I have a plan which comforts me. I shall insist, this very day, that she allow me to be with her when she takes her saved pills. I shall kiss her brow and smooth her scant hair. I'll stay beside her until she sleeps. The last words she hears from me will be love words. This will be our final secret.

At noon on Christmas day, the watched telephone rings. Anne says: "Molly must have taken sleeping pills last night. She left a note and she is not dead. She's deeply asleep. Harry wants to know why she isn't awake yet and I haven't told him. What shall I do?"

"Do? Is anyone there? Besides Harry, that is?" My voice is hiding in my throat.

"No one has been here today because it's a holiday. I told faithful Claudia they'd be all right and that I'd stop in before bridge. I know she planned this and wants to die and I want to respect that wish. But she's *not* dead and I don't know whether to let her . . . let her die, and whether to tell Harry, and dammit, legally I don't know what's best to do. I don't want anyone to try to save her."

"You say she left a note?"

"Yes. On the foot of her bed."

"Could you read it to me? I mean . . . while we're thinking what to do?"

"Why not? It's in an envelope and written on the outside is 'For my dear ones!' in red ink, in strong handwriting. Underneath that, in shaky writing, 'Please, cremation. No services. Contributions to A.F.S.C.' American Friends. Then inside are several sheets folded over and on the outside in blue ink 'Candida, Of course I love you!' Exclamation point."

"Can Harry hear you?"

"No. At least I don't think so. He's hunched over his heater in the living room. I want to go on. The first sheet is in red ink: 'Please know that this is no sudden Christmas Eve decision. It has been planned for a long time, interrupted often. I have no respect for useless old age, just living on and on. The things I loved to do I no longer can—working in my garden and in my home. I feel the decline keenly. I want to go while I still can choose.'" Anne's "choose" is high in crying territory and I note my throat begin to clog when I hear the words "want to go."

"If you'd rather I see it later . . ."

"No, no, I'm all right. 'So, no grieving. I hope you can get together in a good restaurant and celebrate my decision. Please drink to me!' Exclamation point. 'I know quite well how I have failed you in your growing-up period. *I* . . .' underlined 'have learned much from you. Too late, of course. But you survived and I am proud of you.' Next page. 'And you, my dear Harry, we have had an interesting life together, with many problems, but we had fun too, didn't we? Perhaps we never should have married, but see what we produced! The jewelry in the box on the dresser goes to Emily. I wish there were more. Oh dear, I have nothing more to give. I hope all of you will treasure the old pictures and heirlooms. And do take care of Mamacat! So long, dear ones! Molly.'"

I called Molly's letters "Oh Dears," and since Louis and Emily claimed they couldn't read her handwriting, I often read them out loud at the dinner table, emphasizing the lament, until we all laughed and squirmed, hoping inside to snuff that inheritance which took pleasure in celebrating misfortune. "Oh dear!" meant everything was a mess—the environment, her life, the news, her stomach, the garden. "Poor dear" was used mostly for Anne and she liked to list the conditions that evoked her presumptuous pity— no husband, no children, smoking too much, running to overweight, playing bridge. Tragic, she said, just tragic. I always sputtered "Non-sense!" and wondered what she said about me when I was absent.

Anne is softly crying. I feel tears in my throat.

"I made a decision this morning at four a.m., as usual too late. To be with her when she took the pills, and love her. I like to think myself capable of impossible deeds."

"*What* am I to do right now? I can't just sit here looking at her and do nothing. There's Harry and . . ."

"Tell Harry. He focuses very well when given a real event. Then I think you need to call your lawyer and ask him how to prevent legal trouble—for you. Let him give you orders, don't carry it alone. You've done enough. I'll get in the car right now and drive to Berkeley."

"I'm not sure. Why don't you wait a while. I'll do what you say and call you when there's something new." She sounds far away, forlorn. I see the body beside her, faintly breathing, perhaps trying to hear. We should dig a fitting grave for her among her nigella and campanula, the wet oak branches scratching our cheeks as we bend our backs, Harry in his mackintosh tapping pebbles with his cane, water streaming off his blue-veined nose. Mamacat rubs against our legs, sniffs mud, flicks her plumed tail, skitters up the tree trunk. We know her wish and should not wait for death. Molly likes composting and told me a month ago that she would like to climb into the rotting leaves, to decay slowly without consciousness, and be scattered over her garden when she was brown and crumbly and smelled good enough. She turned slowly away from the black plastic covering, squinted at the dying apricot tree. "Perhaps I wouldn't be good fertilizer. All my bad thoughts for so long. But oh . . . to be *useful* again!"

MOLLY WENT TO THE HOSPITAL. Harry sat in front of his heater and said he didn't want to go, he didn't believe Anne had it right, she wouldn't do that, no she wouldn't. A note? No, she didn't write a note, no he didn't want to see it. Louis, Emily, Jack, and I had Christmas dinner at a restaurant built beside 100-year-old live-oak trees. There were potted poinsettias spotting the room and I wore a red silk blouse and large gold loops in my ears. We raised our wine glasses and drank to Molly but it didn't seem quite right to say: "May your pain soon be over," so we said nothing. Silently I said: "Please let yourself die, please Molly" and was giddy with the first sip. We were merry and talked pointedly of the lives at our table, each of us careful to let every sentence be completed, especially mine. The turkey was tough as stale bagels but no one complained.

OLD HARRY SLUMPS IN THE FRONT SEAT of Anne's Celica, his herringbone hat with the rust-colored feather at odds with the stubble on his chin and neck. Beneath his raincoat he is wearing a black and white print pajama top and rumpled gray pants. He closes his eyes against the harsh sunlight. His gnarled hand grips his cane and from the backseat I can see his red left ear begin to slide into his dirty coat collar. How difficult it is to spruce him up, to keep him from resembling the winos outside his former office in San Francisco. Urging him to shave, bathe, put on clean clothes, wear shoes, looks like pride and contempt, which I feel but don't want to feel, or let him see. His startled innocence ("Oh? Do I smell? Am I dirty?") shames me. I want to remember his tobacco-scented, rumpled tweed suit, his careless hat on wavy white hair, the quick feet rushing off to work, the spearmint gum in his jacket pocket, the coins he jingled when he used to pace and argue. When did he resign?

Anne pulls up in front of the hospital and flicks her cigarette out the window. She can't park here. I urgently want to get out on the sidewalk and help my father exit from his low seat and begin his journey to Molly's bedside, but I'm trapped. Anne waits in the driver's seat and I want to scold but want also for everyone to behave perfectly and for there to be no blame in anyone's heart. He does quite well without my assistance and patiently stands, leaning on his cane, while I squeeze first my legs, then my shoulders through the crack left between seat and doorframe. He looks up and smiles encouragement. I don't know this man whose behavior leaves no opening for my habitual irritation. Suddenly I'm glad he's wearing his fleece-lined slippers and his pajama top. Comfortable feet and soft cotton against a spiked heart certainly make more sense than whatever correct hospital attire I have in mind.

"What's the room number?" Harry asks Anne.

"It's 691. Up the elevator to the sixth floor and then you have to walk about six blocks. Maybe they have a wheelchair. I'll be back as soon as I park."

We have to climb down a long staircase to reach the elevator. Harry clings to the brass rail and watches his feet. I want to leap ahead of him, scoop him up in my arms, be brisk and strong. I want to hurry to Molly's side, or wander forever through the halls and never find her. I gallop to the bottom of the stairs, punch the elevator button, and search the corridor for a loose wheelchair. Why does the hospital think only healthy people visit the sick? I look up at Harry descending step-down-step-together, like a three-year-old, and wonder if our places were ever reversed. Did he wait for me or impatiently carry me downstairs? Why doesn't he ever tell me about that child? The elevator ascent is so smooth and swift we're both surprised when the doors open onto the sixth floor.

The windows along the endless hallway are at head height and the sun is hot through thermal glass. There's a skyscraper under construction with immense orange and blue arms reaching into the light. Numbers on the wall—600–699—with a golden arrow. Harry squints at the numbers and places his crooked hand on a railing.

"Shall I look for a wheelchair?"

"Christ! 691 must be this way. I don't think I need a wheelchair."

"I'll look for one anyway. I'll ask someone. Are you all right? I'll go on ahead and be right back." He doesn't answer me. He's concentrating on getting there, carrying with him a seriousness I'm interrupting with my interest in ease of transit. I walk swiftly down the long empty corridor, hoping no one notices my avid glances into each room as I pass. I see white sheets, old heads sunk into pillows, legs hoisted on pulleys, tubes, hanging inverted bottles, and everywhere black and Oriental faces peering at charts, brown hands holding clipboards, thermometers, limp boney wrists. The air from the rooms is cool and fresh and I wonder where it's stored. The right side of my body is hot, the left side cool, and I turn in place to acquire a mix. At the corner, where the numbers curve away from the window, I pause to lean against the sill and look out at the workers on the scaffolding. A woman stands next to me, in a short hospital gown and booties. She speaks without looking at me. "It's a nice view, but fresh air coming through a dangerous open window would cheer me up." I see the trees down below sway in the breeze and a worker in orange T-shirt on a narrow beam shakes with the force of his drill. I'm almost sure I feel the thud-thud in my feet but can hear no sound. I remember leaning out the hospital window after Louis was born, yelling to Emily on the ground below, throwing her a white winter chrysanthemum.

I turn away to follow the numbers. There are offices and nurses' stations, and then a jog to the right and another long corridor with thermal windows. On the wall there's another golden arrow: 670–699. It's high noon and I can see all the way to the end. I could roll a ball and hit nothing. I don't want to peek into more rooms, especially Molly's. Surely Harry needs me, perhaps is exhausted, can use my shoulder to lean on. I turn around and run past all the openings, around the corner, and when I see him trudging towards me, with Anne walking slowly behind him, I want to stop him and ask permission to be excused from his reunion with Molly.

"Did you see Molly?" Anne asks.

"No, I didn't go that far. I was afraid . . . It's hard to breathe in this place."

"Are you going to faint?" Anne watches me, her eyes remote, veiling contempt. But perhaps I'm seeing what I think I deserve. I'm a weak sister, a disappearing daughter, a jogger in places where everyone walks. She expects me to go sit in the car, or pass out, or get a headache, or vomit, or perch on the fire-escape until it's time to leave. Where *is* the fire-escape?

"No—I'm all right. I'll walk with Harry. You go on ahead."

"Oh—" The arm that lifts towards Harry's hand is bone draped with mottled swaying skin. Her brown eyes swim in pink and yellowish clots. He bends over her head and his lips touch her cheek while the two misshapen hands, his and hers, twine and squeeze.

"Dear heart! Dear heart!" he murmurs.

"Oh dear! I messed up. I failed. Isn't that so?" She stares at him, almost smiling.

"No, no," he says. "You didn't mess up. You never do that. Everything you do is all right with me. It has always been all right."

"Oh you! But I'm not where I thought I would be." She turns her head to look at me. I lean across Harry's shoulder and kiss her forehead.

"Hello Molly. I'm glad you're back." I'm not glad she's back, but am greatly relieved that her messing up hasn't soiled her brain. I pull up a chair for Harry and stare at the black woman in the bed on the opposite side of the room. Her head is a strange shape and though her eyes are staring at the ceiling, she doesn't seem to be conscious.

"Mrs. Gavin, I'll leave you now for a short visit with your family. Lunch is coming soon." Molly looks over at the white uniform, up, up, slowly to the plump black face.

"You! You were the worst torturer! You had all your black filthy friends down in the basement and you wouldn't let me go! You stuck something in my vagina and now I'm probably pregnant!"

"Molly!" Anne gasps. Me, I check out. I move into my observer place and watch that serene black face not receiving, not even smiling wanly at the crazy patient's words.

"You were asleep a long time and had dreams. Now you are awake and you have your family here." Me? Family? Not I.

"She's a nigger liar! I was *not* dreaming! I know what happened to me in this place. Harry, I *know!* Her name is Mary Beth but it should be Mary Death! She's the ringleader." I glance over at the comatose patient to see if her eyes have moved. Surely if she's alive she'll rise up now to defend her sister. She does not move. Harry, his hand still clinging to Molly's fingers, has bent his head and is rubbing his eyes. Anne puts her arm around Mary Beth and asks to see the doctor. They turn their heads away from the bed and Mary Beth pats Anne's arm.

"Don't believe her! She let me sit on the floor for hours and *hours* and when I tried to climb out the window to escape this hell-hole, she twisted my foot and bruised it. I'll show you later, when *she* leaves!" I stand at the end of Molly's bed. A black orderly approaches. He smiles down at Molly.

"Good morning, Mrs. Gavin. I'm Eula's husband. Remember Eula, who took care of you for so long? I work here." Harry offers his hand and we all mutter astonished greetings, fluttering praise of good Eula.

"Eula? Eula? Her husband? Oh, the one who stole my vitamin pills, took them right out of the bottle and stole them every day. They're very expensive, you know. That's why she did it."

The chorus says: "Sorry, no she didn't, we know she didn't, we know how much she cared and how hard she worked." He hasn't stopped smiling and tells us he understands. Mary Beth, Anne, and Eula's husband (after cranking up the bed and smoothing Molly's covers) fade out of the room, leaving me standing in position, waiting, for an eclipse, an earthquake, thunder. Molly is staring out at the sun shining through the curtains. Harry pulls her chin towards him and says: "Molly, I love you. I want you to come home."

Dr. Sasaki tells us that Molly can go home in a few days. He cannot estimate the damage wrought by the pills she consumed. He hopes he has helped the family by feeding her fluids but not administering emergency measures to save her life. He does not smile and doesn't appear to be able to.

I find a wheelchair for Harry and feel very pleased to guide his chair down the long corridors, into the elevator and out, arriving somehow on the opposite side of the hospital at ground level. In the car on the way home I say to Harry: "I have three nice things I want to say to you."

He laughs. "Yes. Go ahead."

"First, you said to Molly, everything you do is all right with me. Second, you said, Molly I love you and I want you to come home. And I can't remember the third." He laughs again. "Oh yes, I remember. You didn't tell her she was saying dreadful things."

AFTER SEVEN DAYS' MAINTENANCE IN THE HOSPITAL, Molly returns home by the same means by which she left: two strong young ambulance attendants, after maneuvering cleanly through antique end tables, around plants and portable electric heaters, past TV sets and the desk in the hall with the blue telephone, gently transfer the old woman from a stretcher to her new bed with aluminum sides that clang when raised or lowered. They feel icy when I lean over to kiss her. She says: "This is an interesting place. How did you find it?"

Claudia, Eula's successor, plumps her pillows and while feeling for a pulse, sets her straight: "NOW MRS. GAVIN, YOU KNOW THIS IS YOUR OL' ROOM AN' THE BED IS A MOD'REN ONE. IT GOES UP AN' DOWN AN' HAS FENCES SO YOU WON' FALL OUT AT NIGHT." She bends to kiss Molly's wide brow and says she's going off duty but will be back tomorrow morning and start fattening her up.

"Who was that?" Molly asks.

"You remember Claudia. She's running things around here and has stored your bed in the upstairs bedroom. She's half my size and lifted the mattress by herself." Believing Molly will hear me, I speak softly.

"But where did she find this room? She's so clever! It's a nice room. I can look out at the garden. In the other room I had to turn my head."

While we gaze out the window at the late afternoon sun lying low on bare plum branches, we hear Mamacat's plaintive cry. I open the window and she sniffs the air and backs up, the fur on her tail separating rays of light. "And Mamacat, even in the dark, found her way to this new place. How clever she is too!"

"I'm just as clever as Claudia and Mamacat. I was so sure you'd be in this room that I stole flowers—orange calendula and poppies colored ferric red, like dark blood blossoms."

"Oh Candida. So beautiful, so beautiful. But you shouldn't! You'll get caught and then what?"

"Then I'll admit I've been raiding the gardens at night because I have a black thumb and the super hybrids make my invalid mother smile, and they'll let me go. Do you want supper or do you want to sleep?"

"It's morning, why would I want supper?"

"Then have breakfast, your bran toast with marmalade and tea with honey. A chocolate truffle for dessert. You're hearing me just fine. Are you wearing your hearing aid?"

"No. I think they stole it. Claudia called them fences, but they are *railings* and I don't like them. Harry will saw them off."

I AM LYING IN BED UPSTAIRS, in a room that is safe and warm. There are windows on three sides and a narrow staircase which neither Harry nor Molly can climb. The bed is known, having been mine in childhood. The headboard is scarred with my initials, which I accomplished by pressing into the soft wood a new thumbnail for which I would receive fifty cents when it attained a certain length. The wood is lighter around the letters, where Harry must have tried to sand down the sin and did not do a good job, perhaps didn't want to. Whenever I lie on this bed, I travel easily to other rooms, into houses with footsteps and angry voices. In this bed, I read a book cautiously, uneasily, aware that I am escaping. I grow stiff with listening. I sleep fitfully and dream of fires, earthquakes, arriving at school naked, missing my streetcar, not knowing the answer to a question, fleeing across an open field in my black panties and bra, my legs stumps without feet. I dream of getting caught (stealing, poking a finger into my hole, not wearing my glasses, bleeding through my skirt), of animals being cut up by men in white lab coats who slice from whisker to tail without spilling blood. Children are lost, girls are found battered, raped, lying in ditches. When the mockingbird sings, I try to perch in the tree and utter derivative sounds.

"I HOPE YOU SLEPT WELL LAST NIGHT," Molly says. "I don't know how you could have with all that went on last night up there. I'll *never* forgive Harry for what he did." She has more color on her cheekbones and is trying to wipe the butter from her fingers with a blue paper napkin. Her long stiff fingers move slowly.

"Harry? What did he do?"

"He tried to throw Mamacat out the upstairs window. I had to hobble up there and wrench the poor animal away from him. He was wearing his plaid bathrobe. It was outrageous! A terrible thing to happen on my first night here! I don't know what was in his mind!" Huge amber tears are oozing from her eyes and as Harry shuffles into the room, she turns her head away and dabs at the tears with her greasy napkin. He leans forward on his cane and I'm afraid he's going to topple over the railing. His eyes and nose are red.

"I did *not* try to throw Mamacat out the window. She was already outside. All night."

"He did. I saw him. I stopped him from injuring her."

I tighten the belt on my bathrobe and sit precariously on the loveseat, newly placed against the wall opposite the foot of Molly's bed. It's a living room loveseat and again I marvel at Claudia's superior ability to make arrangements without miring in family custom. I sniff Pine-Sol and notice that Molly's room now has the odor of sanitation and surgical tubing. The sewing machine has vanished and with it all the garters, pincushions, spool boxes, and clothes to be mended. One bureau has been moved out from under its gold-corded, hanging mirror and placed against a wall six feet away. The mirror drifts forlornly above bare floor. A TV has been set in front of the mirror above the second bureau and angled so that Molly can watch. A remote control is propped against the bed railing. The unframed Matisse print has lost one of its thumbtacks

and the yellowed paper curls. There are no piles of *Sunset* magazine, no newspapers, no rubber-banded stacks of bills, no purse,
no journal lying open on her counterpane. That's what she called
it and when I was small and sick I used to study the criss-crossed
pattern of my blue and white coverlet and wonder about its name.
On Molly's bed is a white cotton sheet that is covered by a large
white beach towel. My stolen flowers, poking up out of a cracked
yellow pitcher beside the TV, look foolish.

There's been a cultural earthquake in this room, I think, and
try to erase "cultural," take it back, because I know it means black.
Yet I wouldn't think of interfering with Claudia's march towards
function, sterile surface, convenience, away from memory and lost
ability. *I* am not bandaging Molly's widening bedsore or insert-
ing a catheter to catch urine in a little plastic pouch at the end of a
tube pinned to the mattress. *I* am not changing her bed or lifting her
to a wheelchair for a ride down the front steps and on out into her
winter garden. I am not even here to settle my parents' quarrel, if that were possible. They inhabit a region of deep time,
and although I'm a sliver higher up in the road cut, I am no different
from Mamacat. They acquired me when? After Anne, before
brother Barry. I grew and began coming in and going out the
front door, with or without a man or flowers, in anger or neutral,
with one child, then another, sick or well, needing money or not,
staying to eat supper or saying I had to leave, bringing a dog, a

friend, something to be stored in the basement, driving a different car.

I used to be a part of their living history but am now a railing, a faded Matisse, a closed journal, a beige bathrobe with red trim. I hear Anne open the front door and shout hello. I should warn her but I cannot move. Soon she stands between Harry and the bed and the scene looks tiny, far away, as though I were viewing it from the last-row balcony, and I hear her say: "Mamacat is just fine. She's out on the porch sunning herself." Harry is leaning his head against the wall. Claudia pushes past me, catching the fold of my robe and exposing my bare knee. I see bone beneath the brown skin and hasten to cover my secret.

"MRS. GAVIN HAD A NASTY DREAM. SHE WAS 'TACHED TO A TUBE AN' DIN'T GO NOWHERE LAS' NIGHT. BATH TIME, SWEETHEART." The white of her uniform blinds us and we stare. She lowers the railing and the metal clank pops my ears.

"GOTTA GET THIS ROOM WARM SO SHE WON' CATCH COLD!"

Molly smiles and tries to unbutton her nightie with stiff fingers. Harry turns and places the back of his bent finger on Molly's cheek. His cane falls to the floor. He says: "Oh dammit to hell!" Anne picks it up and hands it to him. He says: "Thank you, dear." We follow him into the hall, linked to his dragging steps, respecting his sorrow, loving him, hating him. I hear: "Oh Claudia, I will feel so much better after my bath. They *never* bathed me at the hospital!"

MOLLY REMAINS ATTACHED to her tube for six months. She never speaks of her hospital nightmares, and perhaps has forgotten them. Harry is once more her "dear heart" and she frets about his diet, his sloth, his posture, his refusal to "go out and see someone." She greets me whenever I arrive and seems to be listening when I speak to her. Our conversations often stall at my end.

"You are looking *thin* and tired," she says.

"I'm not tired and I weigh the same."

"Emily took care of us last weekend and she was lovely. She is so pretty and she handles Harry just right. Where did she learn that?"

"I don't know, certainly not from me."

"We had an exhausting party and she made new curtains for the house and so many people came and stayed and stayed."

"When was that?"

"When she announced her engagement."

"Emily?"

"We're talking about my dear sister, not Emily. She's marrying Walter, her persnickety, persistent beau. I don't like him at all."

While I lapse into sorting time present from time past, a dead sister from a live granddaughter, I'm tardy in noticing that she is trying to get out of bed, has in fact pulled the pouch at the end of her tube up into the bed. It is deep pink in color rather than the golden I expected.

"Why is it pink? Shouldn't it be yellow?"

"Why is what pink? I've talked too long and I *must* get up and get dinner started."

"Wait Molly, Bruce is fixing dinner and Harry and I will eat in here with you."

I pull the sheet back over her legs and reach under to extract the plastic bag containing her sunset waters. It's time to check Claudia's careful RECORD OF PATIENT CARE which sits on the kitchen table, remote from blood and wound, an abstract document that includes all dosages of medication, each time of bandage change, every gram of food consumed, every bowel movement (consistency, color), every slovenly act of the night attendant, and each refusal by Mr. Gavin to cooperate with her orderly procedures. She begins each entry "Mrs. G." or "Mr. G." and thereafter calls him or her "the patient." "Mrs. G. passing more blood today, even clots. I called Anne 2 p.m. She will call Dr. B. Karen! You must rotate Patient before you leave! Decubitus widening and bleeding some. Proper care can prevent it!!" I place my finger on "decubitus" and look around me. Bruce is rushing back and forth from oven to sink, wearing tight jeans, a green and blue plaid shirt, and his ridiculous red and white checked apron looped around his neck and hanging to his knees. Harry is sitting on a stool in the corner, apparently asleep with his white stubbled chin on his chest.

"Harry! What does decubitus mean?"

"What? What? No such word."

"It must mean something. Claudia wrote it on this report."

"She's an ignorant, bullying, tyrannical crone. No such word."

"It means bedsore," says Bruce, pausing briefly in front of us, his fingers wrapped around a dripping lettuce head.

"What do *you* know about it?"

"Not much, Harry. Just that hospitals say decubitus because bedsore is descriptive and depressing."

"Go look it up, Candida. Probably related to recumbent, same Latin verb. Claudia is half savage, half machine."

Although I lean over Harry's immense Webster's dictionary in his den and turn the pages, I don't turn on the light. I know he's right and will tell him so. I sit down in his rotating chair and try to avoid the squeak. On each visit to this house, this is the only room where I can find peace. I know Harry never comes here anymore and that stamps are to my right, letter opener to the left. The thick blotter has dents where the legs of his Underwood used to sit. In this room I sniff work smells, pages of typescript and newspaper decaying in drawers, cigarette ashes pressed into the grain of his desktop, the dry death of moths against the naked 100-watt bulb of his red metal lamp. Behind me in the dark are the high shelves filled with his reference books, which he used to check his flawless memory, a memory for lines of Shakespeare, Montaigne, Homer, Horace. Four volumes of *Authors: Living and Dead* up there, and amongst the Gs, no Gavins. I want to feel sympathy for a man whose wife is dying, for a father whose children don't love him, for a writer not even granted a footnote, and can find only grudging respect for his accurate disinterment of a Latin verb. What did he say to Claudia the other day? I hold myself very still and try to remember. Bleak House? No. "Black House," he said, smiling, "you are turning my house into Black House."

MOLLY LIKES TO HAVE both her daughters in the room with her, and on my last visit to her bedside, Anne and I stand before the color TV, oohing and aahing at ice-skating duets set to Russian polka music. We talk during commercials and make little attempt to be heard, having tacitly agreed that it is not possible. Molly says: "I am the obbligato to your happy conversation," and she smiles, pleased with her elegant sentence. Later that evening, after Anne goes home, I sit on the loveseat and write Molly's statements in my red journal:

"I wonder if Anne will attempt a rescue. She won't succeed. We're all in this together."

"Harry *must* get a motorcycle. I've decided that. We'll get one tonight."

"Oh *why* am I so particular in the cleaning? It doesn't make a damn bit of difference!"

"Candida's face is very red. I wonder if she's brought a fever home. Wicked of her."

"Oh Candida! How clever you are in finding me each time!"

MOLLY DIES ON JULY 3. Karen, the night attendant, writes in Claudia's Record:

> 7/2: Mrs. Gavin at 11 p.m. called me. Said she felt
> wird. She said she want to talk. I said I wud call Mr. G.
> but she said no, didn't want to talk to anyone, just talk.
> I held her hand and she said I was lovly. She said she
> saw pink lines in blue air, blue like the perfume bottle
> in the window. She said she was very happy and knew
> evrythin was different now. I ask how different and
> she said the pink lines was runnin out and she was lyin
> in soft blue. She asked me if workkin and goin to
> school was hard and I said no. P. fell asleep at 12 p.m.
> after rotashun.

Anne makes all the arrangements and says there's no point in my driving to town since there would be no funeral and no memorial, at Molly's request. I talk to Harry on the telephone and the first day he says: "Mother was old, very old. It was time she died. I told the newspaper my mother had died and had been quite sick for

172

a long time. They'll write a good obit and that's that." The second day he says: "Molly's dead. I don't see how I can go on without her. She was a wonderful, wise, sweet woman, your mother. She suffered a great deal these last months, but we had a good life together. Poor dear Molly."

Tabu

A week after Molly's death, Anne says: "I shall *not* care for Harry in the same way. I want to get back to my house, my cats, my garden. I don't want to see him every day. I want to go to work and go home at five."

She is hunched over the kitchen table, fighting tears, and although Anne never loses control in a big way, I'm afraid I may for the first time hear her scream. I lead her into a feverish discussion of "What *are* we to do with Harry?" What does *he* want? Can't be left alone. Have to reduce costs. Have to sell house. Which costs more, health attendants 'round the clock or a nursing home? Might set fire to house if left alone overnight. Wouldn't eat. Bruce will have to continue fixing dinner. For one person? Should have companions. Nursing home? Will he go? How do we feel about putting him out of his house (home) and into a home (institution)? Is there any money left? How long will it last at present rate of spending?"

Claudia is coming in and going out, washing a load in the machine, drying it in the dryer, scrubbing death from Molly's room. I know she's listening but I'm grateful for her presence and am sure that Anne, finely honed as she is to business and family crisis, will continue talking calmly until we have a plan.

"What about having a caretaker move in here?" I ask eagerly. "Then we wouldn't have to move Harry, or sell the house. We could stop thinking about a cruel, sterile nursing home—the idea, the guilt. How about Claudia? She lives in an apartment, too small she says, with her husband who doesn't work. They could live here together. She could garden, or maybe he knows how. And she wouldn't have to commute to another job where someone else is dying." I am hurrying to escape, and want, before I go, to put people in niches, to set the feet of strangers on the polished floors. Molly's beloved colors are fading, her perfume, the light is too bright, Harry's pretending he's blind, he's too polite and accommodating. I must hurry. My plan is humane, psychologically and financially sound, logical, amusing. Puts Harry where his liberal mouth has been, places daughters back into their own homes, lets air into closed boxes.

THE INTERVIEW WITH LARUE AND CLAUDIA as prospective house-tenants takes place at nine a.m. the following day, a Sunday and Claudia's day off. Harry is wearing shoes and has let me comb his hair. He has been up since six, taking a shower, shaving, setting his teeth on his gums with Fixadent. Claudia knows it's okay with Larue, Anne and I know it's okay with Harry, Harry knows it's okay with his daughters, Bruce has said it's okay with him. I'm drunk on plan, discussion, agreement, the miraculous merging of everyone's self-interest. It's National Brotherhood, Sisterhood, Familyhood Week. I'm ready for Harry's puns and would like to sing "Kumbaya" with our hands joined.

Eight-fifty-five a.m. Harry and I are smiling at each other. We sit together on the sofa, our feet placed confidently on an immense circular rag-rug which must have taken the maiden aunts all their lifetimes to complete. A brass bowl filled with summer fruit glows on the oak coffee table. Autographed first editions line the mahogany shelves. As Anne opens the front door, I see a large volume leaning against the floor lamp, on its cover a black warrior, his face striped crimson and white. I hustle it off-stage into a glass-doored built-in next to the fireplace, and flip it face down on top of Michelangelo's David, which decorates another book of inconvenient size.

Goodmornin', what-a-nice-mornin', on-our-way-to-church, may-I-introduce-Mr. Gavin-and-his-daughters, this-is-my-husband-Larue. Claudia is wearing pale blue chiffon on top, the ruffles draping her bosom, her strong arms, her waist. The skirt is a vertical cylinder, a vase for the blouse, and tilting daintily on the brown rag-rug are black patent-leather sandals with faceted heels (like Indian arrowheads?). Over her right arm, a white beaded purse hangs from a tortoiseshell handle. Her wet coral lips and white straw hat convince me she's sent her younger sister to our garden party.

Larue steps forward in white patent-leather loafers. He shakes hands all around. His hand is dry and bony and I say glad-you-could-come, we-appreciate-Claudia-so-much. There's a strong odor of cheap perfume in the room, the kind I call Tabu which always enters the corner of my left eye, rises to brain, sinks to stomach, produces nausea, headache, and an anarchic depression. I link this scent to first dates, weddings, church, airport restrooms, check-out lines in supermarkets. If there ever was a first time, I don't remember when that might have been, and never have I fought back. I should say: "Your perfume is making me sick," but don't. I huddle in a corner of the sofa and clutch a small pillow to my stomach.

Larue sits in a chair opposite Harry and when he smiles I see his gold teeth shining next to white molars and brown skin. The men talk football teams. Where would they be without black athletes? Harry asks, and then goes on to say that he thinks Berkeley is probably a pretty good place to live, compared to the South. I begin with the patent-leather shoes, move up to silky lavender stockings showing below gray polyester crease. His lavender sleeveless unbuttoned sweater, draped elegantly against the white-white shirt with gold cufflinks, confirms my sense of personal anarchy. Anne lights up and offers her brand. Her arm is white.

Claudia digs into her beaded bag and pulls out Camels. She offers one to Larue. Larue nods towards Harry and Claudia says oh-no-he's-a-good-boy-he-doesn't-smoke-anymore. My stomach coils and again I study Larue's scuffless, stainless, creaseless white shoes. Clouds of Tabu and smoke settle on my shoulders as Anne speaks of price and room arrangement, who would sleep in which room, and would the upstairs bedroom be left free for out-of-town relatives who might want to spend the night?

That would be me, a dutiful middle-aged daughter arriving to visit her good boy father, bringing flowers, hoping to smell furniture polish, listening for the sound of seventeenth century music from the radio hidden behind crystal sherry glasses on a brass tray. I imagine plastic flowers, Aretha Franklin or big band sounds, Larue coming out of the bathroom in his bathrobe, a six-pack on the sideboard, a velvet, iridescent picture of a dead president on a wall, unemployed relatives (our fault) lounging on the brown sofa, a lavender plastic spread on the oak coffee table, chicken frying at noon, Pine-Sol on the toilet paper, Tabu in the drapes, cigarette butts in jar lids on every table, sticky gray smudges on the blue telephone.

There's no doubt about it, Harry is enjoying his guests. He's laughing at something Larue has said, pointing at the bookcase with his cane, saying "Too damn much! I've read too damn much! Who gives a goddamn! Get some life around here. My grandson, he likes books. He can take them all. Put different books on the shelves and I'll sit here and stare at them. My wife, wonderful woman, she died you know, she was always telling me to read, wanting to know what had happened to me that I didn't anymore, always telling me something awful she'd just read and sticking the article next to my chair. Read about the lake dying, the animals being cut up, the poisons in our food. I didn't want to hurt her feelings. Literature is stench, someone said."

He utters this last quite cheerfully, as though he were commenting on having a good dinner. If my head were not in a C-clamp, if my stomach would get off its pogo-stick, if Claudia would sit down, if Larue's smile didn't shine so, if Anne hadn't just offered refreshments (coffee and croissants), I would point out that even his condemnation of a life's work is a quotation. Something has gone wrong. For the working out of our plan, Harry must resist. If we don't have to coax, shove a bit, how can we know we are justified? Yesterday, when we cautiously presented our thoughts, he said: "Yes, yes I think that's a good idea. She's bossy, but she means well and perhaps her husband is someone I can talk to. I could show him my workshop and get some writing done. I don't have much time left."

Now Harry is telling his sixty-three-year-old war stories and Larue responds with twenty-six-year-old recollections of being a soldier in Korea. Harry is listening hard and asking questions about weapons and attitude. "My son went to Korea and that's where he

grew up. He came home healthy and determined to go to college."
Harry leans over to turn on his heater.

"Me, I was so gone on stuff, I don' remember comin' home, jes' remember one day wakin' up in re-hab, chewin' on my wrists."

"Oh Larue, Mr. Gavin doesn't want to hear about that," Claudia says, putting a mug of coffee in his hand.

"Yes I do. I had a friend, a very dear friend, named Jack Black. He was a professional thief who had a lifelong habit. I met him . . ."

IT IS PAST NOON and Anne and I are lying on lounge chairs in the backyard. I lift my face to the sun and through half-closed eyes can see the wisteria bursting from the carport lattice up over the roof, the lavender blossoms hanging down over Molly's windows.

"Two quotes from somewhere," I murmur. "'The house weighed anchor for the passage through the night.'"

"Yes, and the second?" Anne takes a bite of her thick sandwich, which drips pus-colored mayonnaise onto the napkin spread across her chest.

"'The most exhausting thing in life . . . is being insincere.'"

"Right. Did you take some cafergot? You sound fuzzy."

"Oh yes, I inserted a sliver of balm in my rear two minutes after they left and now I'm recovering nicely. We're not going to let him have his way, are we?" I close my eyes and watch red streaks shoot across a dark-brown curtain. I hear Anne's sigh and the faint sound of a paper napkin, rhythmic, insistent.

"I don't believe he knows what he wants. The nursing home is a good one. And dammit, I'm tired of having to think about it. If he stays here with Claudia and her husband, I'll have to . . . oh I don't know what might happen . . . I . . . just . . . don't know."

"Do we have to consider it further? Why can't we just put him in the nursing home and sell the house? Didn't you say that was necessary? Why did we let ourselves get so confused by the Claudia and Larue plan? Why, why, why?" I sit upright and glare at my sister who is calmly clicking her cigarette lighter and watching the flame bend in the breeze.

"You can ask why all you want, and perhaps later on we'll discuss it, but tomorrow morning, I am taking him to the home. Could you go back to Santa Cruz and get the truck? I want to furnish his room with his own things. What you can do now is help me explain this to him. I don't expect him to argue."

"Right. Good decision. Just give me five more minutes in the sun."

HARRY SAID HE WASN'T GOING TO GO through "another god-damn Christmas," and two weeks ago, on the fifteenth of December, after lunch at the nursing home's assigned table, he lay down on his freshly made-up bed, and died.

Natural Attractant

My hill house is up three miles of winding road past the mom 'n' pop store; one mile in the other direction you're on the freeway. My nearest neighbors live two turns down the lane and I don't know them. The postman leaves my mail at the store. I have a telephone, water from a well which fills from a spring on up the hill, and electricity most of the time. The utility wires are strung somehow from the place which holds my mail. I don't understand how and have never cared to learn.

Yesterday I had a dog but they killed her. At dawn, her bark plunged into a dream, sharp with alarm, then muted, strangling. The sound seemed to come from just beyond my bedroom door and I knew I'd have to scold her because she was an outside-at-night dog, faithful guardian of home and mistress. While I slowly pushed my arms into my bathrobe, my feet into my shoes, out my window I could see the apron of summer fog surrounding my car, draping the eucalyptus below, tucking into the valley stream. I was the shrouded drowsy gray queen of my hill, alone at last, having paid my dues. Bless Jack for making this home possible, for dying without suffering, his briefcase open in his lap. Dreamed of his hands and skin again last night. Six months into dream and liking it perhaps better than flesh.

When I opened the bedroom door, she fell against my legs and I let myself sink down beside her. Sweet love, I said, it's all right, you did right, good dog—words I knew would calm her. Blood dripped from her nose onto my garden shoes. She lay down and placed a paw on my forearm. My hands formed a bowl under her nose to catch the blood and I thought she might drink and stay with me. My fingers probed her neck fur, seeking a wound, a hole lodging a bullet which my fingers could pluck. In twelve years she had never been sick and I remember telling myself that all that stored-up health would fight for her. She nudged my knee, staining my beige bathrobe with streaks of red. Her head slid from my lap onto a Navajo rug with black and red pattern. I placed my ear against her ribs. She hated invasion and had always squirmed away from me, standing up abruptly, bringing me a ball. I heard little sighs and groans inside her and she lost size, like a balloon with a slow leak. I gathered her fur against my chest. I said: I'll be with you soon, but I don't believe that. Dead is dead. It's just that I'd often whispered in her soft ear that we'd come out even and I wanted her to know I'd be along shortly. I understood that I did not feel curious about the feet moving beyond my head. Event, time, weather, why didn't they cease? Her quiet, surprised dying heated me.

"Your dog barked. We couldn't let her bark."

Three young men were standing in front of my desk. Three pistols lay neatly alongside the typewriter, blue-black, shiny. My ridiculous BB gun stood up tall in my grandfather's hand-carved desk chair. I had studied my first and only weapon, hoping to learn how to discourage the rabbit who ate the green leaves of new plants. One morning I opened the back window and primed the gun, shouted a warning and hit him in the neck. I ran outside and found a brown trickle of blood seeping into the ground. My dog sniffed the dirt and dug a hole. I emptied the BBs and stood the gun just inside the front door and was planning to take it to the dump. I stared at the gun and the chair until a frame grew around them, ornate with gold curlicues.

A woman was sitting on my window seat. She was older than the men and seemed tired. Flakes of dried clay crumbled from her tan hiking boots and she flicked them onto the floor, slowly, as though practicing her aim. A child stood near the closed front door. His thick blond hair was drawn back in a braid which fell below his waist. He twisted the end until taut, then let it unfurl and began again. I looked into his face as he stared intently at his braid. His lashes were dense, casting shadows on his cheeks. Ashamed? Of the death? Of his companions? Could we make it right with a burial? Children are good at grave digging. They like to ask questions about what happens to the body in the ground. They listen with wide eyes when you tell them about maggots and nature's way of cleaning up and then later, when the name has been written on crossed sticks, and flowers stuck in the soft dirt, they cry and say they hate death.

I stood up slowly and seeing the blood on my hands and bathrobe, I remembered morning duties. I turned towards the bathroom and a young man in jeans and a gray sweatshirt blocked my way. He stared over my shoulder at the woman. Printed in gold gothic on his chest were the words Garlic Protects. I couldn't remember ever having my way to the bathroom blocked by a body. I thought I might ask, Don't I have the right? Would mention of a full bladder move him? I was having trouble believing that these people were in my house. I was afraid to say anything. I had often sounded off at the least infringement of what I considered to be a well-earned solitude and was puzzled by my unwillingness to utter a word. Did I want them to think me mute and senile? Shameless, I bent over and clutched my privates. I don't know what signals were passed but the child moved swiftly. He turned the knob and pushed hesitantly as though expecting to find cockroaches on the walls. He closed the toilet lid and climbed onto the wide ledge below the window. Asparagus fern sprouted around his ankles. He jiggled the window until it settled shut and balancing on his toes, placed a steel rod upright against the upper frame. Where did he get that rod? He jumped from his perch, raised the toilet lid, and closed the door by backing up until he heard the latch click.

The room was small, scarcely large enough for a solitary sitter. With the backs of my knees against the toilet and this small soldier facing me, my robe hem fell across his shoes. They were Wallabys on their last four inches of shoelace. They were caked with clay from the creek-bottom. He sighed, opened his lips as though about to say something, then closed his mouth. His face was smooth and much too beautiful for a boy, but boy he was—I knew. He grabbed his braid and tugged on it, and with his other hand, palm up, gestured towards the toilet and turned his back to me.

He was polite in his monstrous duty, and it was not yet time to speak. I pulled my nightie and my robe to my waist and sat down, carefully arranging the dark-red stains over my brown knees. My waters were shy about coming but I sat on, waiting patiently, and the child stood still, twisting his braid. I thought of Jack and the times I had sat on the edge of the bathtub while he peed, had intruded for the fleeting intimacy gained from breaching one of childhood's taboos. I had watched him shave, naked before the basin, freshly amazed at a face that could grow hair overnight, loving the wildwood smell of his shaving cream, thinking how odd it would be to have a penis hanging down.

I flushed the toilet and ran hot water into the basin. I opened the cabinet and phizzed a mound of Jack's shaving cream onto my face, dimpling the soft foam around my eyes, under my chin. I hoped he would turn around and laugh, then I would laugh and we would begin to make plans. I peeked over my shoulder and saw a stern profile facing the closed door.

I took my time washing, not forgetting deodorant, talcum powder, and gold earrings. I stood at the door with him, like a dog waiting to be let out.

I HAD NOT HEARD A SOUND while attending to morning duties; their feet were Indian feet. The rattan shades were down at every window, even in the bedroom. The kitchen window didn't have a shade and an orange madras spread (mine) was tacked over it with my sturdy white thumbtacks, which meant they'd been in my red Chinese box containing all my clips, cards, and typewriter ribbons. All of the blankets, suitcases, electric heaters, rugs, and my son's cameras and video equipment were pulled from storage beneath the window seat and placed in a jumble on the floor near the body. She was half into a green plastic sack. I didn't want her in a sack and looked at the child to see if he felt the same way. He stared at the wild coyote head with the big ears and I could see he was having difficulty, perhaps with his stomach. He looked around the room, at backs, heads, hands, guns, and when he couldn't find the woman, his eyes tipped up towards the ceiling then fastened on his braid, held tightly in his fist. I don't know that he was looking for her. All I'm sure about is that she wasn't there and that I missed her, if only because she chose to sit on my window seat, my place of peace and body comfort. I had sat there so many hours watching robins in the pyracantha bush. Lying back against the pillows, I had gauged the struggle between the pampas grass and encircled eucalyptus. The tree was slowly pushing new growth to the sun. At night, I could see myself reflected in the glass.

I didn't want to know their purposes. I would walk out the front door, get into my car, and drive away. Let them have the house to store their plans and equipment. I would excuse myself, say have a nice day. I wasn't afraid to sally forth in my bathrobe, but when I took a step towards the door, a man clothed in faded blue-jean overalls pushed a neat pile of garments at my stomach. A gray sweatshirt and drawstring sweatpants, ugly and lumpy, my worst color. I shook my head and tried to walk around him. My shoulder touched his upper arm and was singed. His eyes were blue, gauleiter blue, but his expression said don't-make-me-force-you/I-don't-know-how-to-force-anyone. His lips were slick with saliva; droplets glistened on his beard. I extended my hands beneath his and he dropped the clothes gently. I moved towards the bedroom and was inside before I noticed they'd removed the door. There was no inside. Was that their intention? My bureau drawers were hanging open, empty, and all of my layer-against-skin garments were piled in a corner. My bookcase, which I had thought too long and high for the room, was hidden behind a motorcycle, black with red stripes, alive with shining oil, perspiring a stink of gasoline. Across my bed lay steaming khaki sleeping bags. A very good idea, drying wet stuff on a waterbed. What else could I learn from them?

I selected white panties from the pile at my feet and after a glance over my shoulder at a bearded profile above a farmer's costume, I turned my back and modestly stepped into nylon. The cool embrace reminded me again of Jack and modesty seemed suddenly the funniest notion in all the long history of life. Pants next in a hurry, drawing the waist in and making a knot. Now I was weighed down by garments. I yanked off the bathrobe and let it fall to the floor. I faced the window and pulled my nightgown over my head. Warm below, cold above. Dared I search for the bra? I kicked at the pile on the floor and saw a shoulder strap. I lifted it free with my right foot. This was morning calisthenics, rendering me strong. I bent towards the window, shaping breast to cloth. I hoped they would tell me to hurry.

The gray sweatshirt felt ugly and I looked for beauty out the window. Wet masses of vine framed the view, striped with lines of rattan shade. Climbing baby roses, an invitation. Of course someone helpless lived inside pink roses. More holes appearing in the leaves. Green grasshoppers, each one almost as large as a single leaf, climb sedately at night. I have watched them from my window seat. In the morning, when I search with my rose-care aerosol can, they are nowhere. I looked through a hole as intricate as the leaf itself, to the driveway beyond.

My car was gone.

My car was gone.

Sun slicing fog, steaming the wet asphalt around a dry rectangle.

IT'S DIFFICULT TO PAY close attention to night shapes when a man lies beside you. If that man says he counts a night well-slept if he does not dream, if he reaches for your thigh after turning off the alarm, if he believes your mind is empty because you are silent, the night events escape, the shapes drift. Goodness knows I told him enough times, said I couldn't remember if he kept on interrupting. He said remember later, after he's gone, meaning a daytime gone, not where he is now. Dreams must be enticed, seduced. Old lady, get back into bed and slide into morning again. Perhaps he took the car and you've forgotten. Forgetting a lot these days, aren't you? Going to the Laundromat, then shopping and forgetting to pick up the wet clothes until the next morning. Done that twice lately. You spend your time piecing out dreams, seeing messages in a lizard's tilted eye, a ravaged rose leaf. You fall asleep while wondering about the Stick-A-Fly and what it MEANS. You know damn well it IS, and doesn't MEAN a thing. Remember what it said on the box? It is a non-poisonous, nontoxic spray, NATURAL ATTRACTANT for flies. They stick to the glue on the vertical cylinder. Not only that, flies *like* vertical surfaces, they *like* to go where other flies are. It's fly psychology, very scientific. They call it space-age glue. And I know it's hard to remember, but this fat dream began yesterday when the hummingbird flew in through the open front door and got stuck up there and by the time you'd climbed on the desk and reached up, his strong wings had rescued him. He sat on the window ledge and when your hand closed over his soft body, your lizard eye saw two bird feet glued among the dead flies. He lay on his side in your hand and you said to him, whiz your wings, you don't need legs to fly. You put him outside in a clump of mint geranium and walked away.

I CLOSE MY EYES and invite the dream to enter and surround me, finish the story. I cheat a bit. Instead of sinking back into an odd detail, like the shaving cream in the bathroom, I coax as though speaking to a God. I say: I know you're a big one and have your reasons. I know I've been praising my solitude too much and it isn't decent to be so happy with only the companionship of a dog. I need this lesson. I huff from the outside although I know better, having much experience with exit and entry dream protocol. My eyes snap open again and again, with a little click each time. They stare at the blunt nose of the motorcycle whose headlights are the faceted eyes of an enormous insect crouched against the bookcase.

There's a war going on and I am territory. Motorcycle, strange men, guns, fog, empty drawers, mud, dead dog, a twisted braid, a woman sitting on my window seat—I line them up. I must not concern myself. The dream's mouth will open and swallow. I turn over and bury my head in my gray arms.

My Past Tense

Nicky Baddagliacca told me this story when he was ten,
and the distance between a six-year-old and a
nine-year-old is vast . . . but Nicky has been
shining bright since I met him, age two.

I want to forget what happened down the block three years ago. My parents think that I've forgotten, they tell each other I have, and the biggest secret I keep from them is that I haven't. I let them think otherwise because it's kinder that way. If they knew how much I think about it, every day, even at night in dreams, they would worry. I'm nine now and even after it happened I went on being the wow-boy they'd always thought I was. I was, and am, their darling Nickie. I'm everything they ever wanted—smart, lovable, good-looking (though I'm putting on too many pounds because I *love* pizza!). I'm a friend to my little brother Jeffie, a leader at school, every teacher's favorite kid. (I don't push this; it happens because I am Nickie, the one who has the ideas, draws the best, does his homework, usually obeys, gets along with everyone.)

So you're thinking now, why doesn't he get on with it, quit bragging and tell what happened three years ago? You're probably dreading a story about kidnapping, falling under a truck, or maybe epilepsy, told in whispers. Mom and Dad have even tried to make me feel better by telling me that what happened was *unfortunate*, but not bad like what *could* have happened to me, somewhere, was it?

So I will get on with it, at my computer, in my room separate now from Jeffie's, because I'm the thinker and he's the twitcher, always wiggling and running and playing ball even inside our nice house.

Our house is in a real nice neighborhood, on a cul-de-sac (I know that's French but I can't translate it. I just know it means the street ends at the end of the street). Mom and Dad are very friendly with everyone and everyone likes them and vice versa. No problems. The kids are all about my age and we play outside a lot and invite each other over often and sometimes sleep over. Most of the parents work, both of them, and most houses have both a mom and a dad. Everyone speaks English, and everyone goes to some church. We're Catholic and my dad's from an Italian background, but not my mom. (This sounds like a Who Are You? lesson we got in first grade.)

So one day Mom tells me that a new couple has bought the house at the end of our street. Our street meets the cross-street I walk down to get to the bus which takes me to school. This couple is having an open house on Saturday and has invited the neighbors to stop by and introduce themselves. Mom sits down at the kitchen table where I'm having my after-school milk and cookies, and she says: "They are dwarfs. Both of them." I giggled. (I *was* in the present tense and *giggled* is past tense, and I think that's because I still can't believe I thought something about dwarfs was funny. So I'll stick to the past tense for a while.) Another parenthesis: (I love stuff about tenses. My teacher says present tense makes the action and the feelings more close-up, more like it's not *going* to happen, but *is* happening. My sci-fi would be too scary in present tense. Which is why I'm ducking into past tense, hoping what I say will stay there and quit bothering me. I also love parentheses. They give you wings and you can fly above the story for a while. That's a metaphor. I also love . . . never mind.)

So when she said "dwarf" I remembered a circus TV program where there were little people doing stupid things like tugging on a nine-foot-tall clown's pant leg. Jeffie rolled on the floor laughing at this and I told him it was a stupid show and they must have been cruel to the animals to get them to do amazing tricks and I asked him if he didn't think the clown was more sad than funny. He said: "funny," I said: "not funny, sad," and we threw those words back and forth at each other until what we were saying was funnier than the show.

Mom looked thoughtful and I knew she had more to say about dwarfs. "They're just like other people except they are very small. They were born that way."

"What's that supposed to mean, 'born that way'? When you're born, you're little, right?"

"Now Nickie, you know what I mean. I mean that when they are born the doctor can't usually see that they are not going to grow like normal people. It has something to do with the pituitary gland not working right."

"Can't they fix it?"

"I don't think they can. If they could, they would, because being a dwarf makes it hard for them in this world. We could look up 'dwarf' in the encyclopedia and see what it says."

"Maybe later, Mom. The kids are waiting for me to play ball."

Mom looked at me with that expression that says she means to talk further to me about this or that because she isn't quite sure what I'll do when an upcoming event arrives. I don't cause much trouble for my parents, but when I do, it's a doozy, as my grandmama says. Mom and Dad are good at doozy-prevention. A Nickie-doozy (Grandmama's word) is: 1. crying for a very long time about something. Or you could call it howling, wailing. Example: I screamed for three weeks on the bus when I had to leave my old school and go to a new one. Or, 2. arguing about something done to me that I think is unjust or unfair and wanting this made clear to the perp (one of my new words which is short for perpetrator) and I must receive words from the perp which convince me that he understands how wrong he was and is sorry. (The perp is *always* a boy.)

Sometimes, not as often now as when I was younger, the two

doozies are combined. I'll give you a for-instance. (That's a hyphenated noun which my favorite kindergarten teacher gave me.) One day at kindergarten, Nathan, my best friend, hit me on the playground at recess, and it hurt. He didn't stop and say he was sorry. He just ran off and lined up to go inside. I started crying (not because it still hurt but because of the injustice which I'm big on) and I tried to hit him back, and we went inside to the story circle and I kept on crying and howling and trying to run across the circle and slug him. I also, between wails, argued my just case. I *love* to argue! The circle teacher kept trying to talk sense to me but had to talk above the noise of my cries and she told the other teacher to take me outside to calm down.

I sat on the fir-bark and tried to make so much noise they wouldn't be able to hear the story inside. My favorite teacher, who was outside with me, said: "Stop! I want to ask you something." I stopped crying because sometimes she's got good ideas. "So, Nathan hit you and you want to hit him back, and then he'll hit you harder, and you'll hit him, and you two'll have a war, and he'll put out your eye with a stick, and you'll kill him. Dead. *Then,* will you stop crying?"

I stare at her and I feel a smile starting on my face. I say: "I don't want to kill Nathan. I just want to *hurt* him." And then, I don't know why, we both start laughing and everything, *everything* I felt while I was crying is gone, just whoosh, gone. She wipes my dirty face with a Kleenex, and I feel large enough to go inside again and listen to the story, be friends again with Nathan who is still my best friend. We can keep on saying silly things to each other like "Totally doodical, dude!" and "Rad! Awesome!" and crack up at how funny we are.

(I notice I've got past and present tense all mixed but it works, doesn't it?)

I know you think it's taking too long to get to what happened that day. You're thinking this kid sure can *talk*, on and on, and never get to the point. So here it is. It was early afternoon and we put on clean, just ordinary clothes. Dad and Mom slicked our hair. Jeffie was three and a half and I was six, did I tell you that? We had, and have, straight brown hair with cowlicks. (I've promised myself I'll avoid parentheses, but I have to ask how that swirl on my head got to be called a cowlick. Does a cow's tongue lick in a circle?) Mom held my hand, Dad held Jeffie's hand, and we matched Jeffie's speed down the block to the dwarfs' house. Dad knocks on their door, the door opens, and here they come, the long moments I can't forget.

Mr. Dwarf opens the door wide and Mrs. Dwarf is standing behind him. I call them that because I can't, no matter how many times I hear it, remember their name. Mom nudges me in front of her and there I am standing looking into the face of a person—a creature like a Ninja turtle but UGLY—my same size. I hear "This is Nickie, and this is Jeffie and my name is Bev and my husband is

Frank and . . ." and I stare. He smiles, showing his big yellow teeth, his peanut-size red eyes snap shut then open, he puts out his hand all wrinkled and spotted and I shrink back into Mom's skirt and I push my face into the soft lavender and pink. My knees are water, my arms hug her smell of soap, her safe pillow body. I feel her hands on my shoulders, steadily turning me around, and I begin to sink to the porch step which is covered in artificial, stupid, bright green carpeting. She pulls me upright and I stand again in front of him and he's me in a mirror, what I'll look like when old, still the size I am, never growing, just suddenly old like those computerized photos you see on the missing children cards they put in your mailbox. I know it's me, I have no doubt about that. On this side, I'm gone, not there, not anywhere. I've turned into Mr. Dwarf.

I know this took no more than a minute but a minute is a very long time. The scream came from down around my knees, up through the tube of what was left of me, then out into the air, and I ran, wailing, doozying, down the street, fear chasing me, past all the familiar houses, to home, through the front door, up to my room and into my dark closet. I sat in there with the door closed, shivering and crying, crying, hugging my knees.

Of course they came after me, Mom, Dad, and Jeffie. I heard them downstairs calling: "Nickie, where are you, it's all right, Nickie." Jeffie crawled in and threw himself into my lap, patted my head and said: "Okay? Okay, Nickie?"

(I couldn't help getting into the present tense there for a while. It pulled me in, but I'll try now to stay in the past tense, but no promises.) (And no more parens.)

Dad lifted me from the floor of the closet and carried me downstairs to the living room. He said my face was red and it felt puffy but I'd stopped crying except for a few sobs now and then. We all sat in a row on the sofa. I was cuddling in Mom's lap, then Jeffie looked scared, then Dad. Dad looked worried, sad, and even a bit angry, which I could see in his eyes. Jeffie kept patting me and each time he did it I knocked his hand away from my knee which still felt like water. Mom and Dad talked and talked, sometimes both at the same time. They understood, they said, I wasn't to blame, perhaps it *was* a shock, perhaps we shouldn't have gone, but how could we refuse, wouldn't that have been rude? Then silence. Dad didn't smile at all. He sighed and said: "But Nickie, it *was* rude, you must know that. You are a kind boy, but I'm awfully afraid you have hurt their feelings."

That had not occurred to me. I didn't think of them as having feelings. They were images in a trick Disney mirror, they weren't real. I hate to hurt anyone, or any animal! Dad said they might be *deeply* hurt. And I started crying again, ashamed, and wanting to fix the hurt somehow. Somehow.

Going back to apologize was my idea. This is hard for me to believe but it's true. I said, hiccupping: "Maybe in a little while, while the open house is still on, we could try again. Not try, do it right the next time." Everyone smiled and got busy bathing my swollen face in cool water, cuddling me, hugging me, telling me I was brave and a super kid.

And while the little family was walking down the street again, the same as before, I had something like a déjà-vu, which my teacher once told me about. It was a video re-play, but real. I felt the fear come, and told myself that the first time I didn't feel fear when I was going towards the dwarfs' house so this time it could happen differently. This time I could put out my hand and I'd know he was a dwarf and was not me, grown old, no larger in size. This time I would know we were two separate people, he a dwarf who couldn't help it, who sadly never grew, and I a little boy who would grow as big as my dad, and it would be a long time before my face would wrinkle and turn yellow and my hands would have spots on them like Grandmama's.

I know you can't possibly believe this—I have trouble my-self—but the video went forward just like before and *exactly* the same thing happened. That's where the déjà-vu comes in. Down the block, very near their house, I knew what would happen. I could have predicted it. Because I was caught in it and couldn't stop it. It had already happened and it wasn't happening *again*, but was a re-run of before. Time was stuck there. Nothing different. I didn't get to the apology. It wasn't there on screen. Again they found me in the closet and Dad pulled me out, and the only tiny difference is that he wasn't as gentle.

We didn't talk about it afterwards, not even Jeffie, and haven't to this day, as they say in corny TV mystery shows. "To this day, we have found no trace of her . . ." If Mom and Dad could look they would find the traces inside me. the memory, the shame. I'll never forget, not ever, and when I walk past their house to and from school, I go real fast and don't look. I've read encyclopedia articles about dwarfs (dwarves), and I know lots about the subject, but if he came towards me on the sidewalk, or in a store, the replay would begin. That's what I dream. My forever secret.

Based on Experience

When I opened my eyes, the dream was waiting, as distinct as a photograph I could trace with a finger. I knew it was a dream because when I turned over, the photograph grew smaller and its edges curled up. The backs of my knees were damp and there were cool beads dotting my stomach. I stared out the window at the dripping yellow blossoms of the acacia tree. I opened my mouth and cautiously let air slide into my lungs. As usual, I was brine-packed, crowded by coast fog, but this morning it didn't matter because I would be on the road by noon. Still, getting ready to enter my dream would be more pleasant if the sun were shining.

I wanted to call my daughter and tell her where I was going, but then I would have to explain about the dream and how imagination wasn't enough if you were a writer. You had to have experience. I couldn't be sure enough about details, spotty even in the best of dreams, and that's why I was going. I could hear that cool, young, almost patronizing voice suggesting that jealousy was making me a bit irrational and asking wasn't it silly? She would remind me that what Jack and I had wasn't exactly a one-night thing after nineteen years and ask why couldn't I put my mind on what was in the typewriter and let the foolish man have his fun as long as he loved me as much as he obviously did. Ignoring the part about imagination not being enough.

I pulled myself from bed and walked stiffly through the moist living room. I opened the door and saw the dog. Oh God, I'd forgotten. I might be gone two or three days and I couldn't delay the dream with a visit to the kennel. That wasn't part of it. I'd have to cover the beautiful tan leather in the backseat of Jack's car with a soft cotton sheet and hope that scratch marks would come off with ArmorAll. It was disturbing to think of these details, and how odd "the dog" and "daughter" sounded in my head, as though they didn't have names, names I had bestowed myself and used often, even to strangers.

After a second cup of coffee, I stepped into the shower stall and lifted my face to the warm water. I knew the first thing I had to do was look through the closet for black garments that would absorb the full moon and stars shining on Jack's desert garden. Jack and the woman would be white and I wondered if there was any color in the dream. I couldn't remember but didn't insist on a memory of something that was past and future, all around me. I knew the dream existed in the night and I would stand on the edge until it was time for it to happen.

The ring of the telephone drifted into the water. I turned the knobs and dried myself slowly, hearing and not understanding. The ringing stopped and started again. It would be Jack telling me the airplane hadn't crashed, it was hot (over 100 degrees), he missed me, and asking how was the car? I picked up the receiver and told him I was glad he was safe, sorry it was so hot, and yes I was just out of the shower and would go to my typewriter soon and was writing so much that I might pull the phone and he said fine, go to it baby, I love you.

The drawstring of my black cotton pants scraped my stomach and as I fastened the frogs on my coolie jacket, it amused me to think that they'd better croak now because soon it would be too hot for frogs.

I covered my typewriter with a pink and orange scarf, carefully tucking the silk edges around and under its body to discourage ants and spiders. On a three by five lined card, I wrote down the three tasks for the morning:

1. Remember key to Jack's desert house.
2. Go to bank and buy $150 in traveler's checks.
3. Get gas.

I packed a small canvas suitcase with toiletry pouch and a change of clothes. The clothes I folded into the psychedelic-patterned case were pink. I knew I would not want to wear black when I had left the dream.

Getting ready to leave was easy, requiring only skills and knowledge on automatic. I did not water the garden for it didn't seem to me that time would be passing in any ordinary sense. I closed the windows and locked the door, as I always did when I left the house. The bank and gas station performed perfectly when I said "I want $150 in traveler's checks—in twenties plus a ten" and "Fill it with regular, please." I wrote a check for the bank and paid for the gas with a traveler's check.

Everything was in order and nothing was out of order. The dog lay quietly on the pale-green cotton flannel. The landscape in front and to the sides was unalarming. There were curved hills, jutting oak trees and telephone poles, then flatness and heat. There were many cars and then few. The highway had two white lines or one. The speedometer said fifty-five or sixty-five and every few hours there was a picture of a gas pump in the upper left-hand corner of the dashboard that flashed a yellow light. It flashed intermittently at first, and then grew brighter and stayed on. This was machine talk and scarcely interrupted my necessary concentration on the dream. I always stopped at the next gas station, said: "Fill it with regular and check the oil," gave the dog water in a red plastic bowl, and went to the bathroom. Each time I sat on the toilet, the dream picture went blank and I hurried back to the car.

Jack's automobile didn't know how to cause trouble. The gas-

ket never blew, the radiator kept its temperature, the oil level remained constant, the window buttons raised or lowered glass when
a finger pushed, and there was always water to squirt on the windshield when bugs splattered yellow spokes of light from a black
center. In the door pocket there were useful maps, but I already
knew I had to go south for a while and then east. There was no
need to unfold paper and look at lines and numbers. In the spa-
cious glove compartment were tapes of three kinds: ten Spanish
language cassettes of graded difficulty, four cassettes on How-to-
Be-a-Successful-Salesman, and three exquisite samples of seventeenth and eighteenth century music. On other occasions, I had
felt that sitting small in the huge blue German car was like riding
Jack, but now the dream blocked thoughts that were outside.

I inserted "Hits of the 1720's" as soon as I started my journey.
I played one side and then the other. I wanted Pachelbel's Canon,
which paced my dream, but listened to Albinoni, Bach, Handel,
and the rest, even the side that had no Pachelbel. I liked to wait
thirty-five minutes for the eight notes which told everything, excluding only terror. Six hundred miles, ten hours of Pachelbel on
the half-hour, and when I parked the car on a side street two blocks
from Jack's house, I waited for the notes to curl up against silence
before I punched out the tape and placed it carefully in the plastic
box with the hinged cover.

Before turning off the engine, I pushed each window button
until the smooth electric power had pulled down four sheets of glass

to a halfway point, enough to let in the hot night air, yet keep a dog from jumping out and following me. The orange-blossom scent was heavy now and insistent, unlike the dry, lifting delicacy of my April visit. I pulled a black chiffon scarf from the glove compartment and wrapped it around my light brown hair, pulling the bangs off my forehead, tucking each hair under. My hand brushed one gold earring, hesitated, then swiftly removed the loops and placed them in a tray above the dashboard. The dog's cold wet nose froze a spot on my arm. I rubbed the soft ears, and shivered. There had been nothing in the dream about a car or a dog or walking to the house or using the key which now gleamed in my hand, catching all the light from the moon which was suddenly all around and inside the car. The moon was in it, but I was still outside.

I knew that if I continued to sit, I would begin to think and would miss the entrance. I opened the heavy door and stepped out. The dog jumped into the front seat and tried to get out. I closed the door, slowly pushing the heaviness against the furry chest. The nose poked through the open window and I kissed it and whispered: "Stay."

I stood in the shadow of white-flowering oleander. I felt light and lithe, not at all tired. Through the thin soles of my black canvas shoes, I could feel the press of rough pebbles, black now on the edge of moonlight, but I remembered their daylight color, a rusty mauve, and so light in weight that they bounced when you walked on them.

I walked swiftly towards Jack's street, careful always to remain in the shadow of oleander and olive trees. The house was not yet visible, but I knew that straight ahead one more block, and over one, his corner lot with high white walls on three sides would suddenly be, abruptly, there—white walls with black cypress sentries and iron mandala decoration—and that I would have to go first to the front to see how many cars were in the driveway.

The moonlight was making my black cotton shine and the eight notes began again in my head. The roar of tires and motors on the freeway filled the spaces. I hoped I could step into the dream soon because it was wrong to have noise in the spaces. And foolish of Jack to have bought so close to traffic. There were no dogs in his neighborhood and no one could see behind the walls. There were mailboxes outside the walls but no one ever saw his neighbor taking mail out of a box or said hello, how are you, isn't it hot? Everyone lived somewhere else most of the time.

When I stood beside the white wall, I could hear rhythmic splashing in the swimming pool and knew he was doing his aerobic laps. As I walked close to the white stucco, the fear came and I knew I was entering the dream. The key in my hand was wet and cold. I saw two cars under the grape trellis, the light in the kitchen, and beyond the living room, visible through one of the slender windows on either side of the front door, two white bodies bending over the plastic covering of the pool. The beautiful first of eight was sounding now and silence before the next. My fingers spread to clasp the doorknob. I watched my wrist turn. There had been nothing about a key in the dream, and after pushing the door open, I dropped it in the corner. It stood on tiptoe in the deep pile carpet, like a tiny silver statue.

The woman was standing beside the pool and with quick, short-range movements, she picked up a white towel and a wine glass. She watched Jack as he adjusted the plastic cover and then she turned and began walking towards the sliding door of the living room. She stepped tidily, efficiently, her dark cap of hair bent to one side into the towel held in her hand.

And now in the dream there would be Jack's words and two breasts with dark nipples hanging down, swaying above the black triangle tucked between short white legs.

"Lock the door, will you?" he called out.

I had to wait for the dream. I couldn't go down the hall to Jack's bedroom until the glass door began to slide and the notes began again, but there was no difficulty in trusting. The fear, the music, the picture, all were combining, rehearsed and familiar, but this time real.

The door squeaked and a white leg appeared. Now I could walk on carpets to the golden chair in the corner of his room. There were never any footstep sounds in his house. It was not possible to know of an approach or a departure. In the dream I had known about the lack of footsteps and how dark it was behind the golden chair, out of the path of moonlight which illumined the Super-King waterbed.

I crouched in the darkness, waiting. There was a sound of

shower water and showers were not in the dream. I twitched and sought the notes. Had the dream ended early? If it abandoned me, should I confront them when they emerged? Should I lie on the bed in my black clothes and watch their naked faces? Laugh? Should I pretend to have a knife or a gun and spring from behind the chair? Shower and freeway noise, huge in my head and in the room, absurd sound sucking breath from my throat.

And then the silence again, a silence between and behind the notes. Jack was naked, just as I had seen him in the dream, and he lay down on his back, groaning, his fingers twiddling with the black hairs and flesh between his legs. He pulled and twisted and stared at it. The woman would now walk quickly to the other side of the bed and lie down. Yes, she was walking quickly and she lay down on her side, curled towards his body, but not touching him. She plumped the pillow under her short black hair. He turned away from her and one hand lifted in the moonlight, came down on her white thigh, patted, and she lifted a knee. The hand disappeared between her legs. He and she lay still.

The dream was all around me and the music was streaming through my body, high in my head, low in thighs and the place where Jack had been so many times. He sat up and straddled the woman, pulling her hips under him, aiming. He looked down at himself, at the place where he would enter. The woman watched his face and did not smile. Her breasts parted from each other and there were two moles between.

I watched from my dream. Tiny golden bristles on the back of the chair cut into my hot cheek. He moved with the notes and the folds of his stomach leaked drops of perspiration onto her whiteness. The woman closed her eyes. He was much older than she. Faster and faster and then he cried out, a high wailing moan and "O-O-O baby, bab-e-e" and fell on her.

The noise from the freeway and far, far away, the violins fading in the distance. I had to get up and out of his room. Quickly! They must not see me . . . must not . . . why had I come here? I forced myself to think about the house, the hallway, the carpet. About sleep, and when was it deep? The moon, how long would it shine into the room? Could I wait? The heat. Over a hundred he had said.

I began to crawl, keeping my head below the level of the bed. There was a monstrous fish picture hanging on the wall and he seemed to be watching me and speaking in bubbles. I stopped each time I thought I heard the soft slurp of moving, shifting gallons of warm water. When I reached the hallway, I stood up and without looking back, ran past the spare bedroom, around the corner, and out the front door.

I left it open, and later on, I wondered if they had quarreled about that, and if they ever had words.

Mutuality

Then breathe this strange sweet air
Where touch must speak and see;
The darkness wraps us, layer on layer,
In mutuality.

(from poem by Rosellen Brown, age seventeen)

As usual, the garden hose is not coiled. It is lying across his path from auto to front door, endangering his passage. His suitcases of books and files are too heavy for her to help him carry across the brick entryway, up the stairs, into the house. He must watch his feet. This particular late afternoon he notices that when he steps on the hose there's a crunching sound. He will tell her that if she would coil the hose there would be less water inside it to freeze and perhaps the hose would survive the winter.

There are, however, better things to talk about, and he knows that she's a non-coiler and he's a coiler and reasons are of no interest to her. Long ago she told him that she doesn't like to perform acts which she has to undo and then do again a few hours later, which reminds her of years of housewifery when she felt herself to be inside a film which went forward then backward, then forward again. He's tried the argument that there is an aesthetic in habitually correct actions and she says she likes the idea of beauty in action but wonders if he hasn't noticed how "interesting" it is to oppose the tyranny of habit, the dictatorship of objects.

She joins him in the kitchen. They admire their dog Missy and agree that she is the prettiest, most playful, most loving of animals. Missy inserts herself between them as they hug each other. He begins the preparation of a cup of espresso-au-lait for himself. The coffee machine is pulled forward into the center of the counter; it sizzles, pops, gurgles. She heats water on the electric stove in a small red teakettle, sets the filters (two) into the basket, scoops a tablespoon of decaf into place, waits. They are comfortably silent, gazing down fondly at Missy who is biting their feet and bringing them a dirty sock with a knot in it. The humming computer has been set up in his small office to the right of the front door. The telephone is ringing in his office and on his cordless phone which is lying next to his coffee machine. He doesn't lift the receiver. Her telephone, with a separate line, has not rung, except for his nightly call, for the ten days he's been out of town on business. She steps to the refrigerator to get out the cheese. The blue hand towel, which he says is moisture-resistant, has moved from the upper aperture in the door handle to the lower one. Her hands are damp from rinsing pears under the faucet and when she bends down to wipe, her back gives a warning click. The hand towel changes its position twenty-five times a day when he's in town. She has a reason for placing it higher on the door, but she has not voiced it. They have not argued its position.

He picks up his coffee mug and his phone and moves to the living room. She follows with her coffee and a plate of cheese and crackers. He says: "Christ, it's cold in this house." She says: "The thermostat's up to 70. We've had a most unusual freeze. All the geraniums are quite dead. Also the bougainvillea." He says: "They'll come back." She says: "No, I don't think so. It's odd— the pansies are fine." Missy climbs onto the couch to lick his face, then stretches out across his knees.

She moves to the massive brick fireplace, rebuilt since the earthquake a year ago October, to add more wood and poke with the brass fire poker. He says: "You've become a fire-maker, I see." "Yes," she says, "I like doing it." "It's about time," he says. The only difficulty with tending the fire is that the implement she's wielding has two screw-in parts, the handle and the prong. With use, they tend to come undone. She has to put on gloves and tighten the black hook in the midst of each use. This year, this reminds her of American servicemen and -women in the Gulf and inevitable technological breakdown. She crumples paper (yesterday's *New York Times*) and pushes it beneath the smoldering logs. It flares, spreads flame towards her hands, warms her. She sits back on her heels, pleased with the result of effort, with the timeless, ancient task.

He gently pulls his body out from under Missy. He says: "Sorry sweetheart, I have to go to the bathroom." He kisses the dog's wet nose. She places a paw on his arm to restrain him. On the way through the dining area, he picks up a black leather pouch from the table. He closes the bathroom door behind him. He is not modest but believes that this keeps the warm air which rises from the electric baseboard heater inside the room. He opens the pouch and places three new medicines on the counter. "Christ," he says to himself, "three of these plus one Feldene, all to be eaten with food. And if this doesn't fix my toe, an operation. Three weeks off my foot and the company will fall apart." He walks to the toilet, stands with penis ready, gazes at the print of a watering can facing him. He has never thought this amusing. The book lying open on the tank is Kafka's *Letters to Milena*. He has never read a book or newspaper while sitting on the toilet. Not even with the runs. After an unsatisfactory dribble of urine, he thinks: "Christ, I should get roto-rootered soon again. I can remember when I could spray my name far out in the snow while standing on the back porch." He stoops to the toilet roll for a piece of toilet paper to absorb the drip. She's placed it her way in his absence, with paper rolling from the bottom. He removes the roll and inserts it his way. He smiles. He zips up and moves to the basin to wash his hands. The soap is green, translucent, and he's sure it's useless because it refuses to form suds. He dries his hands on the red hand towel hanging from an antiquated brass ring on the wall to his left. The towel is hanging spread out, casual, open. He removes it and folds it precisely, three inches in width, and re-hangs it.

It's too cold to venture out and they agree to dine at home. He has brought fresh broccoli and white corn, green and red peppers, radicchio. He brings a bottle of white wine and glasses to the living room. "Glass of wine?" he asks. "Just a sip or two," she says. He sits down again on the orange velour couch and Missy is allowed to spread herself over his lap.

"Oh—if only I knew a woman as sensuous as this dog," he moans. "You've said that before," she says, "and I don't take it personally. I would like to *be* Missy, furry, black and white, with a wet nose, lying on my back with my paws limp, brown eyes glistening." Missy is lying thus, her hind legs open wide, exposing the pink-furred peeing area. "A nap?" he asks.

"No thanks, the waterbed is re-heating since the electricity was off most of the day."

"In that case, I'll fix dinner. C'mon Missy, old love, let me up."

On nights when they eat at home he usually prepares the dinner, unless he has gout or has had another knee operation. He takes every item he intends to cook out of the refrigerator, then each necessary stainless steel pot, the vegetable steamer, the dishes and Saran Wrap he will use for the microwave. In steady slow motion, he chops peppers, shucks corn, turns dials for burners beneath steamer and pot of water for corn. This evening he puts the Saran Wrap back into its drawer because there's nothing to microwave.

She does not know how to microwave and doesn't want to learn. He calls her a Luddite because she has three manual typewriters, just in case they become extinct.

While he prepares the food, she sets the table. She sets out two placemats, utensils, clean wine glasses, pink paper napkins under the forks, and mayonnaise, salad dressing, mustard, salt and pepper shakers near his place, plus corn holders for him. She transfers the butter dish from kitchen counter to dining room table. When she has finished, so has he, and they sit down to eat. He says: "The corn is tough," and she says: "Mine isn't, it's fine." He says: "The broccoli is perfect, don't you think so?" He holds a piece above Missy's head and she promptly sits, then chatters her teeth and catches without error, then sits and waits for a second chance at her favorite vegetable. If she sits but does not chatter, he says: "Well?" and she chatters.

She asks him what chapter he's working on. He groans and says he's re-writing the chapter on training within a corporation. He does not ask about her writing because she won't answer. He knows that. They query each other about grown children. Has her daughter left that idiot husband yet? Has her son extricated himself from the coils of the IRS? Has his son recovered from the flu? He shoves his chair away from the table, pours a second glass of wine, and goes to sit by the fire. She clears the table and after running the garbage disposal briefly, she washes the dishes in the sink. They don't use the dishwasher because they are in the third year of scant rain. The 1812 Overture is playing on the small kitchen radio. She says softly: "That's the worst piece of music ever composed. I'm surprised they didn't shoot him." She turns it off. "Awful, isn't it?" he says from his seat on the hearth. After she wipes the drain board, she turns off the kitchen light and goes to the living room. She curls up on the orange sofa and begins reading an article in *Mother Jones* about media complicity with the White House. Missy is lying in front of the fire with her head on his feet. Her eyes follow his hand as it lifts his glass of wine.

He says: "I'm tired. I'm going up to bed. Are you coming soon?" She says: "Very soon, honey. I hope the bed is warm enough." Missy, acute about pattern and language, does not follow him because she hasn't been invited. She reads on, skipping whole paragraphs. She feels she's cheating but is sure she's not missing anything she hasn't known since she was ten. She stands up and says: "Come on Missy, bedtime." She pokes the fire to scatter the logs, turns off the living room lights and walks to the pantry to get a dog biscuit. She goes outside onto the deck to close the gate, gives Missy her biscuit, and enters the house through a sliding door.

Upstairs, he undresses by the light coming from the hall. He removes wallet, keys, change from his city trousers and puts these items on the windowsill. He hangs his pants on the chair's back. Shirt and underwear he lets drop to the floor. He is very tired and has been up since six a.m. Phoenix time. That means it's really eleven p.m., not ten p.m. Naked, he goes to the bathroom. He runs cold water and splashes his face with cupped hands. Blindly, he turns around and buries his face in the blue bath towel hanging opposite his basin. He remembers to spray snore medicine up his nose and hopes it works because he would like her to remain in bed with him and not go to the spare bedroom which she does when he snores. He pees in the toilet but does not change the position of the toilet paper roll because she uses this bathroom more than he does. He places the toilet seat back down because once she fell in in the middle of the night when he forgot. Standing beside the waterbed, he re-arranges the comforter. She likes it turned back halfway; he likes it pulled all the way down onto the floor with only about a foot covering his feet. He climbs under the covers, arranges two pillows under his head, and feels himself sinking into sleep.

Downstairs, she runs the water in the sink until it's hot. She fills a coffee mug with hot water and goes to the hutch to get a small bottle of vodka. She pours a capful into the mug, hesitates, then pours another, and replaces the bottle in the hutch. Hard liquor goes directly to her head, making her pleasantly woozy. She hopes this will ease her into sleep and she won't be kept awake by his snoring. This hasn't been effective lately, but she is trying one more time. The most modern earplugs of a substance that alters to the shape of the ear's interior make her feel she's underground, dead. She likes night noises—the owls hooting, Missy's howling with the yelping coyotes on the next hill, Missy's barking, the echoing barks of dogs across the valley.

With her hands wrapped around the hot mug, she walks to the dark living room. Estimating, because she can't see the dial, she turns down the thermostat to 60 degrees. She kneels in front of the fire coals and stares. The vodka warms her shoulders, her neck, her cheeks. She gets up and walks through the dark house to her writing room, opens the sliding door a foot and invites Missy to bed down inside for the night. "Come here sweetie, you can sleep inside because it's so cold. I'll leave the door open for you." Missy stands on the deck and eyes her suspiciously. Her head is down between her shoulders and she looks like a wolf. Since this is a change in pattern, she's not ready—it could be a trick of some kind.

She closes the door between the writing room and the rest of the house, sets her empty mug on the kitchen drain board, and goes upstairs without turning on the stair light. The bedroom is lit by moonlight and he's snoring, but smoothly, softly, without whistles or vigorous shifts in cadence. She removes her outer clothes inside her walk-in closet, setting the folded turtleneck and sweater on the floor lest she wake him by pulling out a drawer. She closes the door to the bathroom and turns on the light. After removing her undergarments she puts on her white terrycloth robe. While she waits for the water to run hot in her basin (there are two, his and hers) she can't help looking over at the hand towel hanging on the brass ring. Just as she expected, it's again folded neatly, three inches across, which makes it impervious to air, and just below the towel, water is splashed on the tile around the basin. She reaches for her washcloth and dries the area. She turns around and pulls out the drawer which contains the hairdryer. The cord is not wound around the dryer but lies white and careless just as she left it after washing her hair. In the morning, after his shower, she knows she will find the cord perfectly looped with plug tucked under. She smiles at herself for this foolish detective work.

Spreading Noxzema on her face and neck, she watches her washcloth sink in the hot water in the basin. She places her hands flat on the bottom of the basin. The steam rises, her head is hot. She squeezes the water from the washcloth and presses it open on her face, rinses the cloth, squeezes again, and pushes the handle down to release the water. She dries her face on her bath towel and creams her hands and face with Night of Olay. As she is reaching her hand towards the light switch, she remembers "secret parts." Silly term, from Shakespeare, dating from her daughter's infancy. She wishes she could think "crotch" instead. She runs hot water into the basin again, retrieves the washcloth, and gives herself what he calls a "sponge bath." She wonders if a sponge would feel good down there. That's not what he means, of course. Should she get "ready"? Put aloe vera ointment on herself? He likes that. It means she anticipates, he says. She turns off the light, opens the door, and walks to the side of the waterbed. His snoring is muted now, even, steady. She gets in, careful not to roil the waves trapped in blue plastic. "Oh Christ, you're icy. What have you been doing? Your bottom's going to freeze my balls," he groans. "I'll warm up soon," she murmurs.

She is soft and smooth. He wonders if she's prepared and he moves his hand over her hip and down and lightly touches. No. He pulls his arm out of the covers and finds the tube of ointment he's tucked into the side of the bed to keep it warm. He's unscrewing the cap with one hand, fingers busy, when he feels the tube being pulled from his hand. He hears it land on the floor across the room. She giggles. The giggle means she's a bit ornery but not hostile. He heaves himself up off the sucking surface and spots the tube easily in the moonlight. He bends over, feels a warning pain in his lower back, climbs back into bed. He says: "Now sweetie, let me, let me, you know you'll sleep better." "So you say," she says. He knows she means "It used to be so" but he's glad she didn't say it. He squeezes a dollop of ointment on his finger and stows the tube, without cap, in a cranny against the bed frame. Now is not the time to screw on a cap. He gently rubs, loving the feel of her folds, wishing she knew, or believed, that this is what they have now and damn lucky to have it. He's safe now, she's snuggling closer, squeezing him, and he moves carefully, delaying, oh once again how fine to love so the skin, the pleasure of this act:

His skin is moist, hot, her hand rests lightly on his hairy thigh. She listens to Missy's melodious howl, which accompanies the wail of a fire engine in the distance. Wrapped in his old arms, grateful for this comfort, as always, she's falling into sleep, and seeing once again their Missy raising her long nose, turning into wolf on a high hill, answering night sounds she must think are addressed to her.

What Raymond Carver and I

Talk About . . .

Halloween, 1993: I am standing in my driveway at midnight, a mug of hot water, spiked with vodka, in my hands. The moon is full, an owl is whoo-ing, and I am thinking about the day and night of the dead and wishing I could go to Oaxaca and dance on graves, be comforted by cadavers that clank and walk through walls—jolly reporters come to tell us what the story is. I don't believe the dead talk to us, not in Oaxaca, not on driveways in the moonlight, but my dog is wagging her tail and moving towards the tall figure in the oak tree's moon shadow. I hear mumbled words:

Mind if I sit down on that wall? You've been bothering me with all your questions. You sit too. We'll talk.

My questions? You've heard my questions?

No. It doesn't work that way.

He is sitting now on the low wooden wall. He is wearing a flight jacket, a scarf, jeans. His legs cross, his hands rest on his knee. I can't see his face because the moon is behind his head, but I know his eyes because they have looked at me from book covers. I set my mug on the asphalt and move quickly to roll a tree stump over near his big feet. I don't take my eyes off him. I sit down in front of him, our heads now on the same level. I bury my hands in my lap. My mug gleams white in the moonlight, tugging at my left eye.

Then why are you here?

I am here to hear—no, to listen to the story. Notice that I said "listen" not "hear." "Listen" is a fine word and "hear" and "here" in the same short sentence would annoy. Oh my, sometimes I forget that I can't re-write anymore. I loved re-writing.

I know. I'm not sure it's a story. It's a tattle-tale. There's a movie now, called *Short Cuts*, advertised as based on nine of your stories and one poem. Your . . . widow . . . gave permission to the filmmaker and . . .

One film or nine?

One.

It must be a very long film. About twenty years long. Which stories? Say them, if you remember.

"Neighbors" . . . "They're Not Your Husband" . . . "Vitamins" . . . "Will You Please Be Quiet, Please" . . . "So Much Water So Close to Home" . . . (oh, how I love that story!) . . . "A Small, Good Thing" . . . "Jerry and Molly and Sam" . . . "Collectors" . . . "Tell the Women We're Going," and the poem "Lemonade." I have almost all of your titles memorized. I think I'm obsessed.

He doesn't move. I imagine he's thinking about his stories, trying to see his characters move in a movie; he's hearing them speak, wondering what the director has done with the silences.

Yes, but it's not clear to me why you called me.

Did I call you?

There was an unpleasant whirling of the breezes and a foul odor. We—don't smell roses, or lilacs. Scents. To get to us it must be an odor, strong as gangrene.

How much time do you have? I want to be sure you hear . . .

I have no time. Or I have all of time. I've been unable to remember what that word means, but if you feel pushed by time, perhaps you should get to the point. What must I, five years dead, hear?

Oh, this is all very upsetting to me. You, the man, though dead, are beloved—as you wished to be—because of your stories and poems. Your time here with us, and your "time" when all of us are dead, is lodged in your stories, which *move* us, and cause a closing of the book, and a sitting there afterwards—after words—to think, shiver, and then later on, we re-read with no loss of awe, admiration, even envy. Your . . . compassion . . . am I misreading?

I hope not. I tried, but sometimes the characters themselves, their words and deeds, convicted them with scant mercy, and I had to move on. I'm worried now about my characters. I don't want to leave them in a movie. You've been hinting that they've been altered, perhaps even damaged. Tell me, begin.

The location is Los Angeles. The filmmaker says: ". . . we wanted to place the action in a vast suburban setting so that it would be fortuitous for the characters to meet."

But I never lived in Los Angeles. My characters don't live there. Wait—do you mean that a character from one story meets a character in another story?

Yes.

How do they get through the frames?

The frames are removed and they just step in. Sometimes they fly, or go in through a TV announcer's voice. The TV announcer is your grieving father in "A Small, Good Thing." He's not with an investment firm, as in your story, and he's an adulterer. The hit-run driver is not a man, a man who stops and looks back and then drives on. The person who hits the boy is a somewhat drunk overweight waitress from your story "They're Not Your Husband" and she stops to comfort the boy and later broods over her brush with tragedy. Ralph Wyman, the *teacher* from your story "Will You Please Be Quiet, Please" is a doctor at the bedside of the boy in a coma. The TV announcer's father turns up at the hospital after not seeing his son in thirty years. I think he wanders in from your poem "Lemonade" but I'm not sure. I don't remember anything in the movie about lemonade. Oh, ghastly movie! There are more wanderings but I'm just telling you about the shards of this *one* story. Telling you makes me want to vomit.

Please don't. I don't want to vomit, I want to laugh. One of my deep-chuckling-rising-to-whole-body laughs, as memoirs of me have oozed. But I can't. I have to sit here in my back-cover-of-the-book pose.

You are *amused?* How can you laugh when your stories are hacked up, Skil-sawed, desecrated, demolished, vulgarized, sprayed with pesticides, their frames removed, names changed, dislocated, and . . . will you stay right there while I run inside and get my thesaurus for more . . .

If your body abandons my . . . presence . . . I'll be gone too. That's the way it is. Tell me the ending of the story "A Small, Good Thing." The movie ending. I worked so hard, sometimes months, on endings.

Be glad that I love your endings. In the *story*, there's that last sentence—"They talked on into the early morning, the high, pale cast of light on the windows, and they did not think of leaving." In the *movie*, the baker brings muffins to the desolate parents and the grieving mother says: "I'd like to see the cake" and the baker says: "You can't. I threw it away."

Oh my. I think they lost the small, good thing.

Lost it? They murdered it. (I'm distracted by a sudden dry wind that rattles the eucalyptus leaves. The dog goes to the edge of darkness and barks, then lies down again between our feet.) When my dog does that I think always of our famous local earthquake. Did I mention that the movie begins with a helicopter spraying pesticides over all the households, and ends with an earthquake?

I like subtlety. I worked for that in my stories.

Yes, I know that. I have to tell you something which perhaps would only be noticed by a woman, although Robert Coles wrote a long article for the *New York Times* in which he said: "Compassion from Carver, Male Swagger from Altman" and "... the women in the film are degraded, insulted, demeaned, scorned."

Huh? There's a lot of male swagger in my stories.

Yes, your males seem born, hatched that way, but the filmmaker alters the stories so that the *women* seem to be at fault for the males' swagger and violence.

Fault? My characters are caught in their lives. They bump against each other and ricochet off and then back. They can't move very far from each other. Their feet are stuck in one of those humane glue traps for mice, and all they can do is wave their arms and squeak.

Can you stay a little longer while I tell you of your story "Tell the Women We're Going"? What the movie did to it.

They removed the ending with the rock and the girls? I had a hard time with that.

I know, the widow has told us that. In the *story*, Jerry's an assistant manager at Robby's Mart. (In the *movie*, he's a pool cleaner.)

We meet Jerry and his friend Bill at a barbeque at Jerry's house. He has two children and another on the way, and a pool. The wives are in the kitchen cleaning up, the children are outside at the pool. Bill notices that Jerry "is getting to be deep." He stares and doesn't talk. Bill asks if anything's wrong. Jerry suggests "a little run." Bill says: "I'll tell the women we're going."

"A" for summary.

I've been studying these stories. Obsessed. So in the *movie* we meet Jerry outside his house covering his pool-cleaning truck lest the airborne pesticides harm it, and then he goes inside where his wife is having telephone sex with a man, in the presence of the two children. Jerry recoils from her words.

Telephone sex? Now please imagine that I laugh my big-rising-up-through-whole-body laugh.

I do not think it's funny. You will please notice that now whatever else happens in the *story*, in the *movie*, it is her fault. How could it not be? She's enjoying her "job" and Jerry has good reason to be getting deep.

Filmmakers sure do earn their pay. What an imagination! Los Angeles. Okay, so the story has been shot. Dead.

But there's more. In the story, the men go drinking and then drive out to the country where they spot two girls on bikes. They have drunk much beer but have no beer in the car. The girls try to avoid the men. They are trapped and Jerry uses the same rock on both girls. Is that what happens?

That's what I wrote. Summarized.

In the *movie*, there's beer in the car and the girls are *flirtatious*. Bill gives a beer to one girl and goes off into the woods with her. The second girl asks Jerry for a beer. She spills it on her blouse and removes her blouse. A blue bra underneath. Jerry kills her and then there's the '89 earthquake. Bill and his girl watch the murder and the earthquake knocks them off the hill.

Man! I'm thinking that the filmmaker has invented a new film genre: Story Stew. Take a well-known writer, or a somewhat well-known writer, put all or some of his stories into one film, heat 'em up, stir until potato, carrot, turnip, and onion hide from each other, add hot, hot sauce, and serve. Kafka—the bug, the mole, the tunnel, the castle, the hunger artist all in the same film. Animation! You could throw in some Ernest, have it all take place in a clean, well-lighted place.

Profit to the estates of the authors. And the filmmaker. I'm assuming the authors would have to be dead? Do you think a live author would submit?

Live authors are all hunger artists.

I've not mentioned that your stories, in the movie, are never allowed to move from your beginnings through your careful ends. The widow . . . says that in the movie there was no "robotic pandering to the text." The movie dives down and drops bombs on one story, then another, until . . .

A very good woman. Gravy years. I hesitate to ask, but must. My dialogues?

Forget them. Gone. The silences between the words offend the film artist.

Please turn your back to me. And close your eyes. In my present state I shall not remember you or what you have told me. Pour the vodka onto the asphalt. It's not good for you. You said that I am beloved?

You are beloved.

I SLOWLY TURN MY BACK to the moon. The dog stands up and growls—a low, soothing, talking growl. She leans against my leg.

Pacific Heights

Kathy and I decide to walk and talk in Pacific Heights. This San Francisco neighborhood is filled with carefully tended gardens—roses, impatiens, wisteria, bougainvillea, geraniums—and yard workers are everywhere busy with shears, leaf blowers, ladders. Never do we see a child or an owner. We can peer over a fence and marvel at the array of colors, or stare up at four stories of house, and wonder, say to each other, "What do the people *do* in there? With all those rooms? Who *are* they?" We like to climb the steepest hills or the Lyon Street steps to aerobic our lungs and exercise our knees. These steps rise uphill for three blocks and they are crowded all day with the fittest people on earth, water bottles in hand, perfect bodies and skin. While we walk we gossip about other writers, tell each other what we've been reading or writing, and Kathy tells me some, but not all, of her life in New York City with one of the world's best-known writers. She is careful of his privacy, and that he is off-limits is clear.

At the top of the Lyon Street steps, we are standing on Broadway Street, the highest point of the Heights, and we can see tiny sailboats on the blue Bay, a freighter slowly heading out, and we murmur to each other that this city, yes this one, must be the most beautiful city in the world. Kathy asks: "Isn't this the street where someone bought a house for $30 million and it is still being built, not even finished? My mother sent me a *Chronicle* clipping about it. The most paid for a San Francisco house ever!"

"Right," I say, "and there it is across the street! Ugly, isn't it?"

"How do you know that that is the house?"

"I saw the article and it gave the address. 2835 Broadway. So much for privacy. But of course for the rich there's no such thing."

We stand still and stare at real estate, surely the only house for blocks around that is without character or distinction. Kathy nudges me: "The statue! My God!"

How had I missed it? A chrome robot, twice the height of a tall man, shining in the sun, grinning its pointed teeth at me, its bulked-out arms reaching out to me, the hands ending in sharp claws. It stands on a ledge about ten feet above the sidewalk, visible from every direction.

"What do you think of its . . . lower part?" Kathy asks.

Again, I had been so held by the somehow shining eyes fixed on me, I'd not ventured lower down. There they were, the parts, the bulging metal balls and the huge cylindrical penis hanging down between muscled steroid legs.

"Oh lawsy," I say, "let's flee. Such a pretty day and now this. Why haven't the neighbors sprayed it with red paint, or knocked it over, or SOMETHING? They could *organize*, lasso it, bring it crashing down, like Saddam."

We descend from Broadway as fast as we can, down a crooked, pedestrians-only street with ridges on the pavement for our feet to cling to. We go down one more street and turn south on a street with gardens and no yard workers visible.

"I'm not sure why I feel assaulted by that statue, but I do," Kathy says softly.

"Me too," I say, reluctant to utter reasons which would sound so trite, or iterate feminist dogma, or reach for aesthetic reasons, cultural laws (Don't display your id in your front yard), afraid I might shriek or moan.

We lapse into a comfortable but nervous silence. Our long friendship assures us we each know what the other thinks about certain matters and we can spend our infrequent times together quizzing each other on new subjects. We see on the sidewalk about twenty feet away, a tall man bending over to smell each pink rose on a bush just beyond a white fence. He is well-dressed in brown slacks and a tweed jacket, about sixty; he is holding a newspaper under one arm, and his hand is clutching a briefcase of good leather. Gray hair sprouts from beneath a rimmed straw hat. He is absorbed in smelling the roses and we watch him, slowing down in order to take in the sight of a man bending over beauty, needing this at this particular time.

Now we approach him and when we are about ten feet from him, I say: "How good it is to see a man bend to smell a flower," a comment not my style at all, preferring as I do not to make the acquaintance of strangers, fearing not danger but boredom, idle chitchat.

We stop near the roses, we smell a rose on another bush, and the man straightens up to his full height, faces us, says: "All human beings are evil. EVIL. All of them!"

I feel a shot of shock, something left over from Broadway Street, but also specific to this event. I try to evade with a comment: "Oh, surely not children."

"Especially children! They will grow and mate and produce more evil humans!" His eyes spear mine and Kathy's hand is on my elbow tugging me away.

I know he is crazy but also want it to be a joke of some kind. I'm reluctant to leave the scene without resolving or dissolving it, perhaps even consoling an unhappy man. There's a giggle trying to rise in my throat. We are at the corner; he has turned away and is walking in the opposite direction. Out of his sight, Kathy and I nervously laugh, not much, a little. We start to walk swiftly down the hill to a gentle street below and suddenly his voice is at our sides saying: "WOMEN! They are EVIL! They produce the babies and all they do with the young is evil and the babies are evil . . ." He edges close to us. Kathy takes my hand and we run/ walk downhill, twitching our heads behind to see if he is following. He is not, but we don't slow down until we're on the street with the garden workers at every other house and we know we can seek help if we need it and not one of these workers will be stooping to sniff a rose or be carrying a briefcase or wearing good slacks and a tweed jacket, or even speaking English.

We arrive at our cars and promise to write and Kathy tells me I need to come visit in New York City and learn how to avoid trouble in a city.

. . . Gone, All Gone

On a rainy, windy winter day, Martin and I are on Highway 101 heading for Willits in Northern California. Five years ago, when Martin arrived to paint my house, we talked for three hours and let Martin's workers do all the painting. I'm not usually fond of talking, claiming it makes my jaw ache, but on this day of our meeting almost everything Martin said seemed to me to be something I'd not talked about in many years. Why was I a liberal? Would we ever win an election? Why did I live apart from my "husband," or did I? He said he would never invade my privacy but was just wondering. I said I was in favor of invading anyone's privacy for if one stepped too warily onto another's turf, life would be intolerably dull, right? Then when Martin's wife showed up to help him mask the windows I wanted to ask, but did not, why had a rather handsome man married an aggressively homely woman? Martin and I went right on talking while Lily masked windows.

Jealousy couldn't poison the air because I was seventy-two, Martin fifty.

On that day of the house painting Martin admired my beautiful shepherd/husky Missy and brought out his camera. As he petted Missy, there were tears in his eyes and he told me he was remembering the beloved dog he'd run over in his own driveway. Then he said his true passion was photography, and dammit, if only pictures would pay more, he'd quit painting houses. He would take pictures of dogs, of course, sporting events, weddings, reunions, old buildings in odd settings, ghost towns, and only in black and white. Missy was black and white.

A few years passed and by that time everyone I knew had a framed Martin photo of Missy displayed prominently in their house. My "husband" had sobbed—most unusual—when Missy died. Today, in the car, in the rain, I feel Missy's presence and wonder if I'll ever be able to let another dog enter Missy's house and yard and eat out of her bowl. Well, I don't have to choose a dog today, I can just enjoy riding in my own car, with Martin driving, to some mud hole named the Milo Foundation, sheltering 120 dogs and not find one to my liking. We would discuss, as usual, silly subjects.

The childish in Martin is what annoys my daughter and son. He's argumentative in the extreme and loses his temper if he feels he's on the losing side, which is often, then can't let it rest or exit gracefully. He has no grace except in executing photos; when he bends down, holds the camera high above his head, crouches at the level of an animal's chin, all his actions are as smooth and sure as a dancer's. But he argues "positions" as though he's on the high school debate team and his dad might whup him if he loses. He has yelled at me, hung up the phone, a few days later called with a swift apology for past rude behavior and picked another subject to discuss. His nickel.

As we settle in the car, I open a bag of shelled peanuts and offer some to Martin but he declines. In the years I've known him I've never seen him eat. He's very thin and tall and he must have some weirdness surrounding eating in my presence. He drinks diet cola but never alcohol and told me once that he used to drink to excess. Then added: "I do everything to excess. I don't know how to stop, or slow down or moderate, can't seem to learn those attitudes and behaviors."

Today he says: "I don't like to *eat*, but I used to be able to drink a six-pack in an hour, talking all the time, watching the girl, pacing around her couch, then reaching out a hand to touch her, pulling back, running, running down her steps, the path, throwing myself into the car, heading for a tree, hoping I'd crash. Well, that was a long time ago. I wanted to close with her, but couldn't."

I like the way he can drive so steadily in the rain and talk with expression, animated, at the same time. I like his use of the word "close."

"There's a hum in your engine. Hear it? You'd better get it fixed, it might be serious."

"Maybe since it's a Honda, it'll repair itself. Anyway, it must be faint, because I don't hear it."

"I brought some albums with my latest photos. Want to see the one on breast survivors, I mean breast cancer survivors?"

"Not particularly, not my favorite subject."

"Oh that's right, you're a survivor."

"I'm not a survivor, I'm me. I avoided all those groups."

"Well, you shouldn't have. They've done so much to help people. There's even evidence that their circles of prayer have helped women survive cancer."

"I don't believe that. No double-blind studies are possible."

Martin swiftly reaches behind the driver's seat and produces an album. I am impressed by the smooth photos, so clear, not pasted on a page but the page somehow is also part of the photo, a new way of storing photos I haven't bothered to learn.

"You're looking at pictures of a group that meets to celebrate their lives and to mourn those who have died in the past year. There was one, oh my God she was so young and so beautiful, named Heather, and her picture was everywhere. Nineteen years old, dead of breast cancer. Just look at her! It's so sad that she was so young and she died!"

"Would it be less sad if the person who died was not beautiful and was much older, say as old as I am?"

"Oh Jesus, I didn't mean that! But it is, don't you think, sadder when the person is so beautiful and gets dead before she's really lived?"

"Not sad*der*. Just sad, for the parents, relatives. With your logic, if Heather had been thirty, it would not have been quite so sad, right? And if she'd been forty and homely, forget sad and just bury her."

"I'm hoping that the cosmetics company will give me the contract to take all the pictures each year. I think these women are superb, the way they climb over their susceptibility to cancer and gather with others to help them. Don't you think so?"

"I guess so. I can't help feeling they'd be better off running fast in the other direction. Show me another album of something else. Whenever I see your fine photos I remember that I'd like to see a whole collection of photos of hair on human bodies, the patterns hair forms, the swirls, etc."

"Okay. Put that album back behind the seat and bring up the black one."

I place the next album on my lap and begin turning the pages. Hair it is. Woman after woman Heather's age, with dark or light long hair falling, swinging past the noses, eyes, caught by a breeze, flying past an ear. Sometimes the eyes are closed as if the subject is in a trance or experiencing ecstasy. All are women. No men, no children. I wonder if it's worth the effort to explain to Martin that I am serious with my suggestion that patterns of hair are, or could be, subjects for aesthetic consideration, possibly even erotic. I think of the almost invisible blond hair on my granddaughter's little brown arms, the black hair poking out of my son-in-law's sandals, the armpit hair of basketball stars, the patterned hair, so symmetrical, on either side of the spine close to the buttocks on swimming contestants. The hair on Martin, a very hairy man! Even *on,* not in, his nose. So interesting, and rare. Hairs coming out of my uncle's ears, most white, but a few still black. Hair on men's legs, old men, young ones, on their hands, their fingers, and especially, hair poking out of shirts or collars, or on the backs of men at the beach.

"Martin, there are quite a few photos of that casual tendril that has escaped the rubber-band or the ribbon, and hangs down the side of the face. You like that, right?"

"Oh, do I! I sought it and caught it when I could."

"You know, of course, that that tendril dropping down the cheek is carefully nurtured and cultivated, designed to escape containment. The ladies know it's sexy and they work on it."

"I don't think they do, but even if you're right, it's still sexy, isn't it?"

"No."

We are near Willits and Martin begins to fret about the lousy directions given him by the woman at the Milo Foundation. We are now off the freeway and in a maze of unnamed streets. Martin's getting anxious and keeps dropping his cell phone onto the floor near the brake. He breathes deeply. Somehow the Milo voice on the phone guides him forward until we're on a mud road with a small MILO sign and an arrow that helps him decide to go bump after bump until we have to stop at a dead end and a cyclone fence.

We zip up our jackets, don ponchos, root around for our umbrellas on the floor, and I sit in the car while Martin lopes into the bushes to pee. What a guy, couldn't he have asked the person or persons at Milo for a restroom? I hear much barking and see cats, wet cats, cats sitting on top of cars, on porch steps as though sunning on a fine day, cats with thick fur who seem so contented I can almost hear them purr. The rain is now more of a mist and not steady. Martin returns and pulls his camera from the backseat, slings it over his shoulder and says: "Ready? Don't slip in the mud!"

Our guide comes down the porch steps and introduces herself. It is difficult to hear over the barking dogs, but she hears Martin growl: "Oh God. I hate barking!" and she frowns. "Sorry," she says. Quickly the three of us reach the first enclosure—beyond a fence, a tangled mass of dogs of all colors, coats, sizes, all wanting a lick of our hands, attention, perhaps release. They don't snarl at each other and are wet but seem healthy. I am realizing fast that the supply of dogs is vast and no dog even in small degree resembles my Missy. They are all mistakes, imposters. I look at 120 dogs and finally point to one who is not barking, seems calm, is perhaps pretty, and I say: "That one is fine. I'm soaked. Let's get back on the road."

I name the dog Cinder because she is black with white eyebrows and white feet and her Milo name, Sunshine, does not suit
her. She sleeps on the backseat and when we stop at an inn for a
light supper, Cinder stays asleep in the car. Over hot cider and tomato soup we gradually get warm and Martin drawls: "Here we
are in what seems to be the library of an old inn in front of a fire
that is glowing—oh man, I should go get my camera!—and I'm
tempted to tell you what I'm sure you don't want to hear. It's more
jabber about how I'm not making it financially and what's bad is
that it's all getting worse because of what I've been doing . . ."

"Martin, eat your soup, and whatever you have to say, get on
with it. You know I always listen, except when I'm arguing."

"But what if you don't like me after I tell you what I'd like to
tell you and you say you'll listen to? What about that?"

"If you don't get on with it, I'm going to fetch a book from
yonder shelf and sit in the overstuffed leather chair and finish my
soup. Really Martin, you're being childish."

"Okay, okay. Well, we aren't making it with the money I make
on photos and I will not go back to painting houses. I borrowed
more from my fat-cat brother, and then, guess what? I spent most
of it on strip joints."

"On *what?*" I return a spoonful of soup to the bowl and stare
at Martin's eyes, now darting from side to side as though he might
plunge to the floor in a fit.

"You know, places where you can see, and talk to, beautiful

women, and my God, how gorgeous they are, and they really like you and they come right over to you and talk up close, then sit in your lap and wiggle around, lick your face, let you see their boobs that aren't all that covered, in fact not at all, and they *talk* to you, ask about your family, tell you about their own husbands, children, and even . . ."

"They have husbands?"

"Sure. Some of them. Some are supporting families; it's good money."

"How much does it cost to get in?"

"In the last six months I've paid out about $6,000. In Vegas, LA, SF. Out of the $10,000 from my brother, meant to tide us over."

Avoiding looking at each other, we both stare at the flames in the fireplace. I am searching for my sense of humor, or my shock. I don't want to sound like a parent and I know if there's a hint of parent in my voice, he'll explode, implode, throw furniture. He's trying to speak and utters only a hoarse groan from his throat. He tries again.

"You see . . . it's an addiction."

"Yeah, yeah. Have mercy on me, Martin. You are . . . how old are you?"

"It doesn't matter how old you are if you are an addictive . . ."

"Personality. So, taking thousands of pictures you'll never sell, falling in love with every assistant you've ever hired, saving pictures of famous women you admire, like, my God, even Martha Stewart, drinking twenty-five cokes a day, working often through the night to get a job in on time, all of that is addictive, I suppose. Falling for a Heather who died at nineteen? Also addictive?"

"You're confusing me. Some of that is, some not. I drank too much, I couldn't stop without AA."

"Would you see if the nice man at the bar would bring me a glass of Chardonnay while I'm in the bathroom? No—I don't want the wine in the bathroom—you know what I mean?"

Martin jumps up and goes to find the bartender. When I return and slide into the leather chair, I take a huge swallow of wine and then put my hand on Martin's knee.

"Now then Martin, I want you to tell me *exactly* what happens in these places. I want to know what the woman is wearing or not wearing, the music played and by whom, how she approaches you or vice versa, how long she stays, how she gets paid, by you, or the management?"

"Oh Christ! You pay at the door, go in and sit at a table. It's usually like a bar. You order a drink, in my case cola, and then a woman comes over, dances over you. I guess you sort of invite her by looking fondly at her. She undulates to the music. Lap-dances."

"Undulates?"

"Well, yeah, moves her torso around, shakes her boobs, hangs her hair down onto your chest, widens her legs . . . God, it sounds so . . . cheap . . . doesn't it?"

"That's your word. Does she touch you?"

"Yeah, but usually you can't touch her. Rules, you know."

"So, does this happen in a big room, or in a small private room? Are there other people around?"

"There is some available privacy, sort of nooks, but no closed doors. And if you want a private place and she yells, there's instantly a guy there as big as an SUV to protect her. Depending on the size of the joint, there are maybe thirty men, or as few as ten. Sometimes the music is live, in the larger places, or recorded, and it's heavy with the beat. As you'd expect."

"I would? Why?"

"Well, there's a rhythm to the . . ."

"Oh, I see. Her movements . . . wait a minute, what's lap-dancing?"

"I think you can figure that out without embarrassing me by having me explain."

"So, do her movements cause you to . . . have an orgasm?"

"It depends. Sometimes, with me, I just feel so good, on and on, never in my life felt like that, and I don't *want* to finish, I just want it to continue, but she's not going to dance on your stuff forever. She moves away, or goes to someone else."

"Is she naked?"

"Almost. All but a kind of G-string, usually. I hope you run out of questions soon because I'm NOT comfortable answering them!"

"Is there hair on her, I mean not on her head but down below?"

"Now you've gone too far. Really. But no, no hair."

"It's shaved off? Why? Men don't like hair on their women?"

"I don't know, but it's shaved or waxed and you can see the folds, the lips, and once, as this woman was dancing on my lap, I saw, I thought I knew suddenly, where LIFE was, right there inside those tight lips, like seeing God, and I thought I would faint, it felt so good, to see that." Martin points into the fire as though he's seeing a presence walking towards us, and he ducks his head, closes his eyes.

I feel us both retreating and I decide not to ask him if he's ever seen God at the end of a penis. I feel strangely exhausted by the conversation, not by what was said but by what it all *meant*. I settle up the bill, payment for being driven so far by Martin. On the way out to the car, where we let Cinder out to do her necessary tasks, Martin says: "These women, you know, are not sluts or prostitutes. They . . . some of them . . . are in law school. They travel together and visit countries. Many are in school, post high school, and people know what they do and don't care."

I stifle the arguments I might mount, the words that would express a desire that a woman retain something of the girl next door.

Often lately I feel I've been on earth too long, far past understanding many of the adjustments, the new ways boys and girls, men and women, get to know each other. Blowing, undulating. E-mail. Chat rooms.

"She's sweet, isn't she? Cinder, good dog," I murmur.

"Yeah, she's okay. Not Missy, but maybe she'll be fun. Oh, Lily and I haven't slept together for six years. It was wild in the beginning when we were hippies, but that is gone, all gone."

FOR THE REMAINING HOUR ON THE FREEWAY, we are silent. Martin probably feels he's gone too far and his comfortable friendship is shot. Perhaps I'll no longer return his calls. I think about men I've known, including my friend Jack and my forty-two-year-old son. Do they go to such places? Do I want to know? Does it matter? Martin walks me to my front door, says: "Get that car fixed. Could be dangerous. It was fun, thanks for letting me drive you. 'Bye, Cinder. Be a good dog."

I'm in a State

This morning Jack said to me: "Well, what are you going to write today?"

"Well," I said, "you know one is not supposed to ask that question of anyone who writes."

"So," he said, ". . . in general, what are you going to write?"

"I'm going to write something about being in a state."

"What do you mean?—being in a state—California, of course."

"I think the metaphor has fallen out of the language, but when my father titled one of his daily articles, 'Don't Tell Me I'm in a State' and then wrote: 'I know I am but I don't want to be told about it,' he meant . . ."

"I see what he meant but what state are you in?"

"I think I told you *not* to ask me about what I am, or intend to be, writing. Didn't I."

"I'm not asking you about your writing, I'm asking you about the state you're in, besides California."

THE STATE I'M IN IS AN OCTOPUS and the pink tentacles reach down into the past *terra* that I thought was *firma*, stirring the once buried quiet stuff, agitating, letting the long-silent voices cry out to me—"Do you remember?" "How could you have forgotten that?" "Are you sure of that?" On and on.

One person has brought this into my life. His name is Bruce Miesey, and though eighty-four and frail and profoundly deaf, he has walked boldly into my sister's life after an absence of fifty-five years. Back then, they were lovers and then he received a Fulbright and walked away. No goodbye. No letters. She did not complain to me. She never complained about anything. That was my role in the family.

Dr. Miesey didn't just drop out of a foggy sky. He prefaced his visit to the Bay Area from Tucson where he was living in retirement, a medieval historian, with a letter to me, not to my sister (not yet) because he was best friend to my ex-husband from hell (now nicely deceased). He informed me he would visit soon and wished to see all the people he once knew in Berkeley. He sent itineraries, dates, and requests that Jack and I reserve certain evenings for him so that we could recall old times. He hoped we had an extra bedroom. We didn't, wouldn't.

Jack is even older than Bruce, eighty-six in January of this year, and not the least retired. He'll run his company until he drops. His bones are aching but his hearing is good, his mind still capable of complicated thought and memory. We've been attached, more or less, for over forty years.

Bruce (I remember that my Ex called him Brucey and Brucey called my Ex Bobby) packed much into the first letter to me from Tucson, in April of last year. He had been reading my books and Jack's to catch up with us. He knew nothing about us except that I had disappeared with Bobby's two children in 1965. In his letter he said: ". . . you failed to mention something about yourself that surely affected your relationship with the other sex: as I've said for a long time, to many people, you were the most beautiful young woman I have ever met."

Me? What balderdash, hogwash. Not only was I not even close to beautiful, no one had ever thought so. I looked into a mirror, back then, and wished, oh how I wished! that I looked like Hepburn or Olivia or Merle Oberon, or Liz Taylor or Ava! And in my dreams, I sometimes yearned to resemble Lassie or Rin-Tin-Tin. Could Brucey be senile?

In the same letter Bruce went on to tell me about Tig, his fourth and last wife, now amicably divorced from him, in fact living next door with her husband. She is the "testamentary beneficiary" of his estate—no children or blood relatives exist. His estate is apparently two houses—Tig's and his own—

in Tucson. She has agreed to care for him "to the end of my days."

Tig is twenty-five years younger than Bruce and is called Tig because she played the role of Antigone at Bryn Mawr as an undergraduate. I went immediately to my Classical Dictionary and discovered that Antigone was a daughter condemned to death by her father because she disobeyed him by burying her dead brother against her father's orders. For this, he sent her to prison to await death. Her other brother visited her in prison, with someone named Erudice, and they all committed suicide. Tig had tenure at Iowa in Classics when she married and divorced Bruce. Neither she nor Bruce have any offspring from four marriages for Bruce and I don't know how many for Tig. (All this Bruce has revealed in his letters to me announcing his impending arrival in California.)

For a number of reasons, it takes a while for Brucey and me to agree on the summer's plans. I do not do e-mail and therefore we must use the phone or slow mail. His deafness makes him sound like a dying frog on the phone, so the letters come to my mailbox and in each he tells me more than I want to know about his plans for June, July, and August, in El Cerrito, Chico and Mill Valley, where I live, and San Francisco, where Jack and I live. He's a scholar and he details travel intentions, route and conveyance, people he will visit, motel where he'll stay (unless he can stay with us), time of day when he'll arrive, his reasons for going to Chico. He's "bequeathing" to several of his grad students, all of his historical files (his *nachlass*) in two huge filing cabinets. He's driving a 4x4 pickup. He has a Verizon cell phone. This ego-man expands, single-space, page after page. I begin to feel sorry for myself, in my state. Can I duck?

Instead, I crash to the sidewalk at midnight on a walk with Jack and the dog, in front of the Russian Consulate in San Francisco. Jack takes my bloody face to the hospital where they X-ray me and bandage me in a fetching turban-style bandage and then let me go home. A gash over my right eye, stitches, two loose front teeth, and bruises of every pastel hue the following day. Problem solved, now I don't have to *see* anyone, lest they see me.

Meanwhile, Bruce arrives in El Cerrito where my sister Anne lives. He checks into a motel and then makes a dinner date with Anne. Anne is eighty-four, I am eighty-two. She has painful peripheral neuropathy—she walks slowly with a cane—high blood pressure, diabetes, failing eyesight. Her hearing is perfect. I tried to convince the California Department of Motor Vehicles (DMV) that she should not be driving. She's had several odd accidents that she did not report to the police or to her insurance company, and when she collapsed in the parking lot outside Safeway and was taken to the hospital, we all gathered—social worker, doctor, my daughter Emily, and I—at her bedside, and solemnly spoke our message—NO DRIVING. Within a week of Bruce's arrival on the scene, the DMV gave back her license with no requirement that she re-take the eye and driving tests.

Bruce said to my daughter when he requested that she help get a king-size bed for Anne's tiny house: "We are intimate." My daughter raised her hand to her face as if to ward off a pesky fly, and said: "Pul-ease Bruce."

Though my sister is rickety, we are all fond of her. She is kind, loyal to a fault, but we are learning that she is less than honest when it serves her. This shocks me for I'm the one in the family who is a veteran embroiderer on reality's edges.

While we await developments, we try to visualize two eighty-four-year-olds of uncertain health being "intimate." We have questions we cannot utter, repugnances we do not express and are somewhat ashamed of, and we hastily fall back, saying: "Well . . . good for them, right?"

NEXT, A FEW OF US ARE IN A RESTAURANT in San Francisco, a quiet place selected by Jack, where the food is good. I declined and my sister also, but the two children, Louis and Emily, now in their comfortable forties, attend, also Brucey and another historian friend who knew my deceased husband and Brucey long ago. He is eighty-one, also a bit deaf, and although he is an American Studies scholar, now retired, he is emigrating to England lest he lose all control and assassinate our president. I don't get much of a story about this evening from Jack who claims he drank himself through it, but my son tells me that Bernard, our American Studies friend, at one point yelled across the table at Brucey: "BOBBY, your dear colleague, was a psychopath, a pathological LIAR, a lazy phony! And Kantorowicz, the man you both revered and studied with, was a Nazi!" My son was not ready to defend his father, a man he'd not seen since he was five, but briefly wondered if it would be allowed for him to walk around the table and tip over Bernard's chair.

Jack rapped a spoon against his wine glass and said: "Now, now, all of that is old, old stuff. Let's have a civilized evening!"

While I've been hiding my rainbow face, the couple has been progressing in intimacy, so much so that Bruce seems to have moved into Anne's teeny-tiny house, made smaller by the new Costco California King-size bed that leaves about six inches for passage around three sides. Bruce has also been threatening to visit me. My valiant and wise daughter firmly informs him that a visit would not be welcome and that he'll have to wait for an invitation. His other plans are to 1. enlarge Anne's house, or 2. sell the house, then they can spend the "lovely money" on a better house with more room for his six-foot self, in a district where they don't have to double-lock the doors and windows.

When my face is back to its normal color and there's only a small bandage above the eyebrow, I agree to meet the couple for lunch in Mill Valley. I'm not sure I'll recognize Bruce, a man I've seen only once before. I choose the Arco gas station for meeting, not realizing that on a Saturday in summer, this corner will be jammed with cars going to Stimson Beach, lining up at the pumps, access in or out complicated by autos and pedestrians. But there he is, standing tall and thin, and he recognizes me while I'm yet unsure. He hugs me close then runs his hand over my bandage and says: "The woman I remember is almost gone, Anne is all gone." Should I congratulate him for his honesty, slug him for rudeness, try to walk away, faint with shock? Is he the only person on the planet who doesn't know that one says on such an occasion: "Oh! You haven't changed much, still gorgeous!"?

In the parking area of the restaurant, I greet my sister, help her exit her car that Bruce was driving and then am surprised by the degree of difficulty she seems to be having walking ten feet from car to restaurant. Bruce is holding her hand and squeezing it lovingly. She is not squeezing in return and does not seem in good spirits. We seat ourselves and she studies the menu. She likes to eat. Bruce says, looking at her: "Oh, I forgot my teeth. You didn't remind me." She glares at him and says: "How would *I* know if you have *your* teeth in *your* mouth?" He remains cheerful but drops the menu and it scoots under the table. I get up and reach down to retrieve it. Bruce says: "Oh you are still *agile!*" Is Bruce that rare persona who *always* puts his foot into his mouth? Is that his special talent?

We slog through the lunch. I ask questions. Bruce answers in his frog voice. Anne eats and does not reply. She is usually gracious and pleasant, but not now. She seems to be a different person. I decide that I have an appointment and therefore cannot invite them to come to my house for tea. I don't want Bruce to know where I live. He has my address and he can read maps though he claims Anne cannot. I'm anxious to escape and we smile our way to our cars. See you soon, okay? Soon after the lunch, the couple drives to Tucson in Anne's car, with her cat in a cat cage. She calls me to say that Bruce's house is lovely and his ex-wife Tig lives next door and is ever so helpful and nice, the cat is fine. Two days later Bruce calls to tell me that Anne is in the hospital with a spell of minor heart difficulty but I'm not to worry because she's being cared for by his "very fine doctor" and should be back at his home in a few days. He reminds me that he asked my son-in-law, the contractor, Emily's husband, to draw up plans for an expansion of Anne's house, with cost estimates, but he hasn't done this yet. Anne has told my son-in-law that she doesn't want to re-model or spend the money. Would I please also get a Realtor to look at the property for possible sale? I hear all this while tensing my shoulders and back, my ear glued to the phone. He slurs his speech and does not pause for whatever comment I might want to make. I say: "Yes, yes, I'll try . . ." then hang up. This is the first time that "gas-light" flashes through my brain. Bruce has just said, "IF you'll send me Anne's financials I'll be able to . . ."

That day I begin not answering the phone, waiting for the voice on the machine, living in avoidance mode. These events are keeping me "in a state." I seem to be waiting for the proper time to re-enter my daily life. Safely.

When the couple returns from Tucson they settle into Anne's teeny-tiny house and Bruce continues to campaign for a house re-model and my son-in-law stalls him because Anne is not enthusiastic. Several times I see them at my daughter's house and he says three times in one evening: "You, Emily, and your mother and I are the three who love Anne the most and it's only sensible that we make her happy by finding a way for us to live together comfortably." The "sensible" comes out "senshivel" as though the man is drunk. He does like his wine but not to excess. I notice that Anne is sipping red wine, slowly. With diabetes, she is not allowed alcohol, but we don't fuss. We worry and discuss after they've gone home. I announce that I feel them to be wayward adolescents and we should call the house to see if they got home safely.

In this period with Bruce having arranged for Anne to regain her driver's license, we all believe we are now in constant danger of being run down by a red Ford . . . a child lying in the street, bleeding, the Ford plowing into a view window of a neighbor's house.

In the middle of one night, unable to sleep, I hear ". . . love Anne the most" over and over. I am startled into sitting up, turning on the light. Do I love Anne? She is my sister, I've known her eighty years, of course I love her. But *do* I? I count the good deeds she's done for me over my troubled years, her faithful interest in every thought I express, her lifelong refusal of any criticism of me. All this should add up to my loving her but I roam the house trying to define exactly what I do feel about her. Love, what is it? I inspect the soggy wrapping around the assumption that one loves one's sister. I'm cross at Bruce for saying this, assuming it, leaning on it.

Next, the happy couple drives to Chico where Bruce will consult with the grad students who have agreed to accept his papers. The night they return, Anne has trouble breathing and can't sleep. In the morning they call 911 and she is taken to the hospital in "extreme distress." My son and daughter and I visit her in Kaiser Richmond hospital. There, in intensive care, she lies sedated with tubes in arm, nose, one hand, and we're told that she'll be "out" until her heart and blood pressure return to a tolerable reading. We lean over her, pat an arm, say: "We're here, Anne, we'll be here when you wake up." We don't believe she will wake up, we assume she is dying. We are grateful. Her pain. We tell Anne we'll be back tomorrow and we leave.

In a week she's transferred to a convalescent hospital affiliated with Kaiser. She receives all nourishment through a tube down her throat. She can talk but only with difficulty. She hates the place, she says the staff has stolen her "pretty black dress," her money ($50), her jewelry. She wants to go home but until she can swallow she'll need a nurse's care. As usual, she denies having had a heart attack though the report hanging beside her bed lists this as one of the causes of her difficulties.

Without being invited Bruce shows up at my front door. He

sits opposite me at the kitchen table for three hours, talking, talking, talking. I try to converse but fail. I grow numb. He says, somewhat cross: "Couldn't I have something to eat?" I pitch him some
frozen cookies. My head, neck, back, and spine ache. He talks
about his scholarship and how much he loves Anne. He tells me the
evening before she went to the hospital they had a delightful dinner. "She was gay and happy, we killed a bottle of red wine . . ."

I say, in a teeny-tiny voice: "Diabetes, she's not supposed to
drink."

"Oh," he says, "my fine doctor in Tucson says it's all right."

Bruce goes to Tucson for a week and while he's gone we visit
Anne in the hospital more often. She is not happy but seems to be
gaining strength. She can't walk unaided. We get her moved to a
more quiet room. She does not speak of Bruce.

Daughter Emily calls me in the morning: "Mom! Bruce and
Tig are right this minute yanking Anne from the Kaiser Convalescent place, the management is resisting, they want a power of attorney, Bruce told them he is her husband, and has something called
durable power of attorney [he does not]. Tig is helping Anne get
dressed and . . . and I'm trying to argue them down. They asked
Anne, 'What do you want?' 'To go home,' she said. 'Will you release the hospital from all responsibility?' She whispered yes and
signed some papers. They're leaving now. Call you later."

At Anne's home, after she is settled on her bed with the tube
down her throat, there is chaos, shouting, accusing. No one be-

haves well. Bruce insists that *only* water go down the tube (this route is for Anne's *only* nourishment). My son joins the effort to bring something like sense to the gathering. The term "elder abuse" flits through my head. He mentions the drinking and Tig yells, pointing her finger at him: "Are you suggesting that we endangered your aunt's life, you who abused her by not visiting?" "Yes," he says and Bruce yells: "I AM GETTING MAD!"

The Kaiser nurse calls the social worker who arrives and tells Bruce that she has asked Anne in private if she wants Bruce to leave and she said yes. He says he won't, the social worker says he must or she will call the police. A male nurse escorts him out of the house.

I was not there. Had I been there I would have been screaming and yelling too. There are certain occasions when no one *wants* to behave well.

MONTHS PASS. Anne gets better and better but is still needing all-day care. She claims she isn't anxious to see Bruce because he gets very angry at her, and that frightens her, reminds her of our father. He yells at her.

"So," Emily says, "what are you planning to do about that anger, that yelling?"

"Well," Anne says, "I'll have to be extra careful not to make him angry." She plans to visit Bruce with her cat in a box, on a commercial airline, as soon as Tucson weather is 80 or below. Bruce has told her to tell me, Emily, and my son not to e-mail him or write, ever.

She goes again to Tucson, Bruce runs into a car, and Anne is back in the hospital. When she returns to California she cannot sleep and the next morning she again enters the hospital. This time she fades fast until there doesn't seem to be much of her left. She says: "It is ending," and we know that she knows. She wants to go home and she is gurneyed home in a van, and dies twenty minutes later.

THE STORY OF MY SISTER'S COLLAPSE and her romance with a former lover cannot be an A-to-Z account. Like dementia, it wavers, tacks to one side or another, drifts, sends false signals, embraces the present, denies the past, and when we think something is a new development, we remember that she said so-and-so last week and this week she claims she did not say that. Our long memory of Anne was being stolen from us. This memory of a smart, loving, robust aunt and sister is being replaced by a ghostly new person that we won't name but are constantly aware of. The term—dementia—is too final, rude, does not allow that this person is still capable of playing championship bridge, a difficult game. Her mind is dementing, but not always, not consistently.

We have to separate out her inability to balance her checkbook, her complete confusion about what meds to take, when and how much, from her insistence that she has not had a heart attack and has never had any heart trouble. Her dementia, there but not named, confuses us and makes our daily efforts on her behalf tentative and without direction. We allow dementia to sit with us while we talk with Anne, and when we take to our cars and drive home, it sits in the front seat and dips forward and back, never letting us forget its presence.

Dementia, whatever it is, in one's eighties, is a condition that does not depart, does not lessen, will continue with lazy force and scattered focus until one's loved one lies down and does not wake up again.

At her memorial, people said: "Oh, you must miss her so much," and I said: "I do, I do . . ."

I remember her phone number and sometimes I call her and her answering machine says: "Hello, this is Anne. Please leave your name and number. I'll call you back as soon as I can."